Life in
the Soul
Lane

REBECCA RUSSELL

Life in the Soul Lane

**A practical guide connecting you to
your soul through the journey of life**

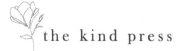

the kind press

Cover design: Christa Moffitt, Christabella Designs
Editing: Georgia Jordan
Internal design: Nicola Matthews, Nikki Jane Design
Author photo: Amy Baxter, ARB Photography

Cataloguing-in-Publication
entry is available from the
National Library Australia.

NATIONAL
LIBRARY
OF AUSTRALIA

ISBN: 978-0-6453444-7-9
ISBN: 978-0-6453444-8-6 ebook

This book is dedicated to my mum, Selena, and my sister, Danica. Thank you for being the other two legs of the tripod. x

Stop acting so small. You are the Universe in ecstatic motion.

Rumi

Contents

Introduction

What it feels like for a girl

What is your first memory of growing up as a young girl? Can you recall the first time that you recognised you were born into this world as a feminine being? Cast your mind right back to when you first learnt what qualities a girl 'normally' emulates, and how she should look and behave. It is in this moment that we establish the idea of what it means to be a girl, a woman, a feminine being.

When did you begin to learn that there was some level of separation or difference between feminine and masculine beings? Maybe you recall being treated differently to your brothers or cousins, or boys that you knew in your neighbourhood. Maybe you were told 'little girls don't do that,' or were encouraged to play with certain toys over others.

Did you have any thoughts or feelings about this? It's likely that you had questions that went unanswered. Did you feel guided by the adults who surrounded you in your life at that time to understand both the synergy and the polarity between the divine masculine and feminine beings?

When we get to school, we go through the motions and the experiences of interacting with other children, making friends with the girls in our grade, and having whispers and giggles about the boys. We begin to explore our nature and our interests. We begin to learn how we are 'supposed' to interact, both with the feminine beings that surround us and the oh-so-foreign masculine beings (especially weird if you only had a sister, as I did!).

If you enter the traditional schooling system, you are obligated to follow a particular curriculum, conform to the school's rules, dress a certain way, act a certain way, learn a certain way. There is not really much encouragement for children to explore their uniqueness, to identify and connect with their true essence. Children are not really taught a lot of information that is going to support them as they enter the real world.

We are not taught how to look after ourselves, and I mean really look after ourselves on a mind, body and soul level. We are not given the space to even discover who we are at a soul level. We are simply encouraged and conditioned to be a particular way, rather than connect to and trust our intuition, or follow our true dreams and desires.

It is through these experiences that we begin to form an opinion about who we are in relation to others by comparing ourselves to them. I think it is fairly rare for a young woman to know who she truly is, or what her intrinsic nature is. We are so entangled in our experiences with others—trying to fit in with our friends and be attractive to the boys—that we really don't have any idea who we truly are. All of these feelings and experiences start to shape who we think we are.

When we grow a little older and are exposed (pun intended) to sexual education, we are not really taught anything useful about ourselves as divine feminine beings (at least, this was my experience). We are not taught of the immense creative power and force that we hold within our womb. We are not taught about how sacred our divine feminine energy is. The essence of what we are taught is how to avoid getting pregnant, and the vague mechanics of our anatomy. And while this information has its benefits, it is just one small fractal of what it means to become a woman.

We as women are deeply cyclical beings, and our energy is vastly different to masculine beings. Can you imagine how life changing it would be for young women to be taught on every level how to harness the power of their feminine energy? Can you imagine what it would be like if young women understood how their menstrual cycle works, the different phases of the menstrual cycle, and how we can support ourselves in an optimal way in each phase?

There are so many things that we could be taught much earlier on in our lives to support us; instead, we arrive in our adult lives still trying to figure out who we really are and how we operate. Knowing this information earlier on would really enable us to move through our lives in an optimal way to support our physical, emotional and energetic makeup.

When we are growing up, we look to our peers, our mothers, our aunts and grandmothers as role models, as measures of who we are, and who we should be as young women. We look to them for guidance; we often emulate their behaviours and patterns because that's what we know to be acceptable or familiar. And while this can be a beautiful way for us to gain some bearings on how to move through life, it can also steer us away from our intrinsic nature.

What would it be like for young women if their elders could pass down their wisdom, nurture and encourage them to be themselves, and show them what they are capable of as divine feminine beings? Imagine if we were guided by our elders through beautiful rites of passage, while simultaneously encouraged to explore and discover our true nature. I truly believe our lives would be so positively impacted if we discovered and connected to our true essence, and identified what ignites us, at a young age. Knowing that we will discover and rediscover ourselves time and time again throughout our life as we evolve and grow.

As we begin to develop into a woman during our teenage years, it can often be a confusing and confronting time. Our bodies are changing, and our hormones make it feel as if we aren't even in control of our own moods or temperament. And we are given only basic information about our impending period arrival and how to prevent pregnancy. However, it is so much deeper and more powerful than that. If you can relate to any of these experiences, then you are in the right place.

The words contained within this book are all of the lessons and wisdom that I have learnt along my way so far about what it means to be a divine feminine being, and how we can fully embody, embrace and celebrate who we truly are. This is the information that I wish I had known earlier on in my life, so that I could have understood and had deep trust and pride in who I truly was. Upon reflection, it had felt as though I was thrust out into adulthood having to discover these tools, practices and lessons for myself—and I'm sure glad that I did!

Turning the pages in this book, you will begin to discover and connect deeply to your true self. You will give yourself full permission to be seen as you are, in all of your glory. There is no need for masks here. Let yourself be seen. Allow your light to shine.

As you journey onwards, you will begin to understand the beauty in the polarity and duality within yourself and all things. You will be at one with the impermanence of all things, letting go of your grip, and allowing yourself to just be who you truly are.

You will gain so much clarity around who you are and where you are going, without being attached to it. There will be practical tips, tools and rituals to support you in moving forward in your authenticity with ease and grace.

My sincere wish is for you to cultivate a deep sense of connection to yourself on every level, be unwavering in your true essence, and find confidence in who you truly are. And most of all, I wish for you to know that you are so worthy of anything that you desire, and have the ability to bring it to life.

Are you ready to get to know you?

Let's do it!

Part I

What does it mean to be seen?

Because you are alive, everything is possible.

Thich Nhat Hanh

I can clearly remember the first time that I really felt seen in my uniqueness. It was when I took the Ayurveda dosha test and discovered that I am bidoshic, with the predominant part of my dosha type being Pitta, followed by Vata (we will get into the doshas later on!). As I read down the list of the traditional qualities of a Pitta type, I was thinking, *Oh my gosh—that's me, that's me, that's me!* Red hair and freckles, check. Hazel eyes, check. Sunburns easily, check. Easily agitated, check. Sensitive to heat, check. The list goes on. But the point is that this was the first time in my life where I felt fully seen in my unique makeup, and there were still more of these moments to come. It was something I could truly relate to in how I felt in my life and my body as a Pitta type, and I could begin to implement tools and supportive practices that aligned with this.

While I was already 'looking after myself' through exercise and nutrition, this was a whole new element of self-support that was unique to me as a Pitta—much different to following a generic health and wellness plan that was designed for the masses.

As I journeyed on, I also discovered astrology and Human Design, which added extra layers of getting to know my unique blueprint, and why I act and feel the way that I do. We are going to explore these modalities in this chapter so that you too can understand yourself on multiple levels.

The true you

On first look, you might have the belief that you are seen. You might relate to and be known for your career title, you might be known as someone's mother, sister, daughter, wife or friend. You might be known for something that you have achieved or how you've performed a particular task. But that's not the true you. It is a part of your identity, but it is not all of what makes up the incredible gift that is you.

Who are you when all of that is removed? Who were you before you became something to somebody else, or before you started to conform to societal norms? When you quieten the noise and tune into your heart and soul, what speaks to you?

I know I have been in this place myself. I worked for a national airline company for twelve years. I absolutely loved many aspects of this job—the excitement of not knowing what was going to unfold each time I came on shift, meeting new and interesting people each day, the beautiful friendships I created with my co-workers, and of course getting all dressed up in makeup, heels and dresses. My identity was so entangled in this job that I had no clue who I was without it. I affectionately call my past self 'the girl in the red dress' because that's how I was known to myself and others for so many years.

As the years went by, I knew that this job was no longer serving me. And even though I was aware of this, and I knew I wanted more from my life, I stayed in this continuous cycle for a few more years. Because I was scared. It was unfamiliar. I didn't know who I would be without the red dress. But it came to a point where I could no longer suppress my desire to follow my dreams, be my own boss and wear bare feet at my desk if I wanted to. I wanted to be free. And I knew that I had more to offer the world, and that my time, knowledge and experience were worth more than a modest hourly rate.

So I did it. I decided to own my worth, take the leap, and have faith the Universe would catch me. And it did. It always does.

Maybe you can relate to this story in your own life—you might replace the career with a relationship, a friendship, motherhood or something else that you have entangled your identity and worth with. But when we start to peel back the layers and tune into our intrinsic nature, we will begin to understand that we are so much more than this.

If this is a new concept to you, it might take some time, love, and patience with yourself to embark on this journey. And it may require you to let go of who you once were so that you can step forward into who you are becoming.

The first step to allowing yourself to be seen is getting to know yourself. The following tools, practices and modalities are ones I have used that have allowed me to connect to and deeply understand my true self, which in turn allowed me to feel seen and embody who I really am.

Modalities to connect to self

Astrology

Despite what you might believe about astrology, it is an extremely deep and fascinating science. While astrology is far too complex to explore in much detail here, I will share an overview of its essence, and share a few examples of my own natal (astrological) chart to demonstrate how knowing our chart can work to our advantage.

According to CafeAstrology.com, 'astrologers believe that the positions of the Sun, Moon, and planets at the time of a person's birth have a direct influence on that person's character.' This means that we will likely embody certain personality traits and behaviours that can affect how we live our life. We are so much more than our sun sign—also known as our star sign, which is what is most commonly known, and where you will find your weekly horoscope readings (is it just me or are they always really vague!).

There are twelve zodiac signs that you are likely familiar with—Aries, Taurus, Gemini, Cancer, Leo, Virgo, Libra, Scorpio, Sagittarius, Capricorn, Aquarius and Pisces.

The date on which you were born will indicate your sun sign. And as we travel through the seasons you will hear astrologers say that we have just entered 'Capricorn season' (I may or may not have picked this as an example because I am a Capricorn sun!). Each season will have its own flavour relative to its sign.

But it's not just the placement of the Sun at the time of our birth that determines our personality. It is also the Moon and the other planets as well, making up the rest of our natal chart. This gives us really good insight into who we are at a deeper level.

The following are known as personal planets, which heavily influence our personality:

- Sun (personality)
- Moon (internal and unconscious reactions)
- Mercury (communication)
- Venus (love and relationships)
- Mars (action)

Other planets and aspects to explore within your chart are Jupiter, Saturn, Uranus, Neptune, Pluto, North and South Node (of the Moon), Chiron, Ascendant or Rising, and Midheaven.

There are also four elements that the signs are broken down into:

- Fire (Aries, Leo and Sagittarius)
- Earth (Capricorn, Taurus and Virgo)
- Air (Gemini, Libra and Aquarius)
- Water (Cancer, Scorpio and Pisces)

Alongside this, each sign will fall in what is called a 'house'. There are twelve houses, simply named after the relative number. This too will bring certain qualities to your character.

Let's have a look at a few placements from my own chart. The most prominent placements are Capricorn (Sun), Leo (Moon) and Taurus (Rising/Ascendent). There are two earth placements and a fire placement, and this in fact makes up the most of my chart. Therefore, I really enjoy being grounded ('earthed') and taking things at a slow and steady pace. I am determined and can work hard. I am driven, with the fire element helping me get stuff done!

That is a very brief overview, but I just wanted to show an example of what parts of a natal chart look like. As you can see, there are so many nuances, so many different elements that make up who we all are according to astrology.

──────────── E X E R C I S E ────────────

Visit astro.cafeastrology.com/natal.php to discover your own natal chart. Read through the report that generates to begin to understand your chart. Notice how much you relate to your chart and reflect on what you can do in your life to support this.

Human design

According to jovianarchive.com, 'Human Design uses your birth data to calculate your Human Design Chart, or BodyGraph. The BodyGraph is a graphic illustration of the energetic flow within your system, a blueprint for how you operate and interact with the world.'

Displayed on your BodyGraph are different centres that are either defined, meaning this is who you are consistently, or open, meaning you can be open to taking on other people's energies or conditioning.

There are five main Human Design types—Manifestor, Generator (including the Manifesting Generator), Projector and Reflector. Each type has its own unique qualities, and similar to the Ayurveda doshas, when we are either in balance or out of balance with our true self in relation to our design type, we will experience either the positive or negative ramifications relative to our type.

Along with the types, there are also what are known as profile lines. These are numbered from one to six. We each have a combination of two lines that form one of the twelve different profile combinations.

So as you can see, even within the types, there will also be variations due to what profile lines we have.

The line qualities are as follows:

- Line 1—The Investigator
- Line 2—The Hermit
- Line 3—The Martyr
- Line 4—The Opportunist
- Line 5—The Heretic
- Line 6—The Role Model

While there are many more intricacies to explore through the Human Design system—far too many to be held within the pages of this book—this gives you a general overview of what to expect when you explore your own design type.

Let's take a look at my profile as an example. I am a Manifesting Generator with a profile line 1/3. My strategy, as it is known in Human Design, is to respond to what is going on around me. My inner authority is the Sacral, meaning that if I can tune into my Sacral Centre, I will receive a really strong response as to whether something is right for me or not. And lastly my not-self theme, meaning negative emotion, that I will experience should I fall out of alignment is frustration.

I also have the profile lines of The Investigator and The Martyr.

One key point that I have learnt about my design type is that I can put in work and effort and show up when I need to, but then I need to retreat and restore my energy. I also need to try things out a little to see if they are the right fit for me. And if something is not working, I should not carry on with it but instead release it and move on.

So as you can see, when we start to explore and utilise

these tools, systems and practices that are available to us, it really does afford us the opportunity to support and fully own our unique makeup.

———————— E X E R C I S E ————————

$$\geqslant 2 \leqslant$$

Visit jovianarchive.com and select 'Get your free chart' to discover your Human Design chart. Do your own reading and research to understand your profile, and reflect on where you can make any changes required to support you.

Ayurveda and the doshas

According to ayurveda.com, 'Ayurveda is considered by many scholars to be the oldest healing science. In Sanskrit, Ayurveda means "the science of life". Ayurvedic knowledge originated in India more than 5,000 years ago and is often called the "mother of all healing".'

There are three energy types known as Vata, Pitta and Kapha, and we all hold these three energy types within us. The whole principle of Ayurveda is based on cultivating balance and taking preventative measures in regards to our health and wellbeing.

These energies are also the three dosha types, and these doshas consist of the five elements—ether, air, fire, water and earth. Vata is a combination of ether and air, Pitta is a combination of water and fire, and Kapha is a combination of earth and water. Depending on our unique makeup, we can either be dominant in one dosha type, two types (bidoshic) or all three equally (tridoshic).

Vata types typically have a tall and thin frame, cold feet and hands, and energy that fluctuates. When in balance, they are very creative and free flowing. Conversely, when out of balance, they can suffer from disturbed digestion, restlessness or anxiety, and weight loss.

Some typical qualities of a Pitta type include a medium frame, red hair, fair skin and freckles. Pitta represents fire, so this dosha type has a great digestive system and eats often. When in balance, Pitta has a strong digestion and appetite, and high energy levels. When out of balance, they may suffer from skin rashes or irritations, digestive issues and a rise in body temperature. Pitta types are also intelligent and great teachers.

Some typical qualities of a Kapha type include a large and strong frame, oily and thick hair, and oily skin. Kaphas are very earthy and often need a little encouragement to get moving. They are also very kind and considerate beings. When in balance, Kaphas are steady, and have good stamina and memory. When out of balance, they can gain weight easily and become lethargic and unmotivated.

As I mentioned at the beginning of the chapter, I am a Pitta-Vata. Studying Ayurveda has taught me what to eat or avoid to support my type, to avoid overheating and to stay out of the hot sun, and that I have a large appetite and need to keep my digestive fire burning, just to name a few examples.

There are so many wonderful tools and practices in Ayurveda, both general and specific to each dosha, that really give us the opportunity to consciously look after ourselves and take a holistic and preventive approach to our wellbeing.

―――――――― E X E R C I S E ――――――――

$$\geqslant 3 \leqslant$$

Visit modernayurvedic.com.au and select 'Test my dosha' to discover your dosha type. Research your specific dosha type and reflect on practices that you can implement to support yourself and your wellbeing.

Practices to connect to self

The following are some of the practices and tools that I use in my life to connect to my true self on a daily basis. You may already be familiar with some or all of them, and I invite you to try them all out over the coming weeks to see how they feel for you.

Not all practices are for everyone, and we don't need to pressure ourselves to do them every day. But they are a great way to connect to self and create an anchor throughout our day. They can form part of a supportive morning or evening routine, should you choose.

Meditation

Meditation allows us to bring ourselves back to the present moment, cultivate stillness in body and mind, dive deep into ourselves, connect to divine source energy, and connect to the subtle energies of our body. There are plenty of scientific studies that prove the vast array of benefits a regular meditation practice has. If you've not yet taken to this practice, this might be a nice opportunity to start exploring it.

The ultimate goal with meditation is to sit alone in silence, with an elongated spine and a deep, even, rhythmic breath. There are many meditation techniques available, such as working with a mantra or visualisation.

If you are new to meditation, you could listen to guided meditations to assist in focusing your mind, or seek the support of a qualified meditation teacher. Not all days on your meditation cushion will be easy, but it will certainly be worth it in the long run if you can commit to a regular practice. You will find several meditations throughout this book relative to the topic of each chapter.

These are my top tips for getting started with meditation:

- Meet yourself where you're at with the level of knowledge and experience that you have around meditation.
- Be realistic with how much time you can dedicate to your practice each day. If you force yourself to sit for thirty to sixty minutes but it's not realistic for you, you will feel rushed, pressured and like

you have 'failed' if you don't follow through.
- Don't get caught up in what your practice 'should' look like or feel like. Do what feels natural for you—that's what is most important.
- It is imperative that you are comfortable for your practice so that you are not distracted by discomfort in your body. It's nice to sit up on a cushion or prop so that the hips are a little higher than your knees. Try using a wall at first to support you if you need to.
- Find a quiet space where you won't be disturbed. This is sometimes easier said than done if you have children or live in a shared space. Have a conversation with those that you live with and explain the importance of your practice time. They will be supportive of you!
- If you feel you need support for your practice, use guided meditation to start to help bring focus to your mind. As you become more familiar with meditation, the ultimate goal will be for you to sit without listening to any guidance.

———————— E X E R C I S E ————————

Begin to explore and implement a meditation practice if you've not already done so. Use the tips just mentioned to support your practice. Observe how you feel in your practice and any resistance that may arise. Find a rhythm and routine with your meditation practice that will allow you to keep it as a regular part of your life.

Mindfulness

We have the opportunity to be mindful in each and every moment. Mindfulness really is a great way to practise present-moment awareness—to be conscious of the way we speak, the actions we take and the way we live.

It might take some time to adjust if you're not used to practising mindfulness, but you could start by catching yourself anytime you are caught up in the future or the past, and bringing yourself back to your present reality.

Being mindful can really help us put things into perspective so that we're not getting too caught up in either the past or future. You can make each moment of your life a small celebration, rather than mindlessly moving on to the next thing.

──────── **EXERCISE** ────────

Make a conscious effort to become more mindful in your everyday life. Notice when you are not being mindful and bring yourself back into the present moment. Notice if there are any patterns or activities that aren't supportive of mindfulness.

Journalling

There are some people who are avid journallers, and some who aren't, or have not tried it before. I was not always into journalling; it is a somewhat recent practice for me. Journalling can be a great tool for accessing our subconscious mind and allowing the words, thoughts and feelings to flow through us and out onto the page. It's also a great way for us to keep track of things that we have done or achieved, and how certain things have impacted us, as well as identify any patterns that are playing out in our lives. We can even identify any fears that might be blocking us subconsciously.

Writing things down in this way can serve a therapeutic purpose. It can allow us to process thoughts and emotions, and gain clarity and perspective around things that are happening in our lives. You will find several journal prompts throughout this book relative to the topic you are learning about.

SOUL REFLECTION QUESTIONS

Begin to explore your journalling practice and see how it feels for you. Use these prompts to help you get started in relation to this chapter's topic of what it means to be seen. Ensure that you are being honest and authentic with yourself while writing.

- How do I currently feel about putting my true

self out there to be seen?

- What steps can I take to support myself to feel more seen?
- Where am I currently not allowing my true self to be seen?

Conscious breathing (pranayama)

Conscious breathing or breath work, known as pranayama in yoga, is the intentional control of the breath. The first part of this Sanskrit word, *prana*, means 'life-force energy', while *yama* means control.

It goes without saying that pranayama is an extremely powerful practice to incorporate into your routine. Our breath is the essence of our entire being. In times of stress, you may hold your breath, or your breath will become shallow, or your breath rate will increase. By consciously breathing, we can calm the nervous system and drop into our parasympathetic nervous system (our rest-and-digest state).

——————— E X E R C I S E ———————

Try this breathing exercise—begin by finding a quiet space and a comfortable seated position, and close your eyes. Take a few moments to still yourself and connect to the natural rhythm of your breath. Take a deep inhale through your nose for four counts, hold the breath for two counts, exhale through your nose for four counts, and hold for two counts. Repeat this cycle four times, and then return to your natural breath. Observe any shifts in your energy or nervous system.

As you progress in your practice, you may wish to explore more advanced breathing techniques.

The chakras

Chakra is the Sanskrit word for wheel. We have seven main chakras that are 'spinning wheels' of energy located in different parts of our body. Each chakra has its own colour and qualities that align with it. It is a common occurrence for one or multiple chakras to become blocked or stagnant for varying reasons. This is why it is important for us to be aware of and nurture our energetic system—because to maintain overall wellbeing, we need to have our energy flowing freely throughout our body.

Throughout the book will be chakra meditations that are relative to the chapter topic and will assist you to maintain the flow of energy in these centres. We are first exploring the throat chakra.

Throat chakra

Our throat chakra (Vishuddha) is the hub of our expression. It is located at the throat and represented by the colour blue. This is where we can express our truth. We can say what we mean, and mean what we say.

Often, when we are afraid to express our truth, our throat chakra can become blocked, and it could manifest physically as a sore throat or loss of voice, as examples. We want to keep our throat chakra open and flowing so that we have the courage to speak our truth always.

Some ways to stimulate the throat chakra include singing, chanting (the traditional sound of *om* is a beautiful place to start) or yoga poses that open the throat.

Throat Chakra Meditation

Begin by finding a comfortable seated position in a quiet space and closing your eyes. Bring your awareness to your throat—feel the energy inside it. Observe without judgement if your throat is feeling open and flowing, or if it's feeling closed and blocked. Visualise a blue spinning wheel of light at your throat. Visualise and sense that the energy is flowing freely inward and outward from your throat. Repeat to yourself three times, either aloud or internally, 'I am safe to express my truth.'

These tools, practices and modalities really were the permission slip I needed to fully embrace parts of myself that I was already connected to, but had not yet fully embodied and embraced. Once I began to honour these parts of myself, I was able to come back into alignment with what I desired and where I was going. And from that place, I have been able to call in people and opportunities that are aligned, because I am now operating in an authentic way.

You will likely have some of your own activities that

allow you to feel truly connected to yourself. Maybe it's dancing. Maybe it's cooking. Maybe it's something completely different. But whatever it is for you, ensure that you are prioritising it in your life so that you can really fortify your connection to self. When we are deeply connected to our true selves, we give ourselves permission to be seen as we are, which is such a beautiful gift that we can give ourselves.

EXERCISE

Do at least one thing each day that allows you to connect with your true self. Ensure that you prioritise this and create space in your day to enable it.

CHAPTER 2

Outside of the box

And the day came when the risk to remain tight in a bud was more painful than the risk it took to blossom.

Elizabeth Appell

I have always felt outside of the box. When I was growing up, it was considered 'normal' to finish school and go to university, get married and have children. And while that is a perfect experience for some, it never felt right for me. When I finished high school, I did not know what I wanted to do. All of my friends went off to university and I pondered how they could possibly already know what they wanted to do as a career. I chose instead to enter the workforce while I 'figured it out'. After a few years of working, I did decide to go to university, however

I only made it halfway through my degree before taking an extended break that is yet to be ended!

Because I had been in the workforce for a few years, going to university full-time felt like I was back at school again. I felt constricted and conflicted about the path that I was heading down. I started to question my motives for pursuing a university degree.

I came to the conclusion that I was beginning to conform to this societal norm of obtaining a degree, and my ego wanted to be validated by my proving to myself that I could do it. So I stepped away and gave myself permission to be 'different'. And once I did this, I was able to connect to what I wanted to pursue.

I have always held a strong interest in health and wellbeing, so this is the direction I headed in. This led me to obtain my personal training, yoga teaching and life coaching certifications. These felt a lot more aligned for me, and the study methods and delivery were more flexible, which allowed me to feel a greater sense of freedom, rather than constriction.

Alongside skipping university, I have also not had the desire to be married or have children (controversial, right?). As I have travelled through my twenties and thirties, all of my friends are getting married and having children, but does it bother me? Not at all. Because I can still be happy and excited for them, while also knowing that it is not written in the cards for me.

I had a similar experience while navigating my teens and early twenties as I never wanted to drink or experiment with drugs. Did I receive peer pressure to do this? Yes.

Did it mean that I missed out on experiences and was excluded because of it? Yes! But I am so steadfast in my beliefs and knowing who I am that it does not bring me any discomfort.

Becoming comfortable with being different

Perhaps you can relate to this story, if you have felt pressure from external sources to pursue something, be something or have something that you know intrinsically isn't right for you. I think we have all felt this, given the society that we live in where there is not much room for individual expression, thought or feeling.

But what if we dared to be different?

What if we became comfortable stepping outside of what is considered 'normal' and choosing our own path? In doing so, we inadvertently become a trailblazer. When we give ourselves permission to be different and pursue our dreams, we inspire others to do the same. It doesn't mean that it is always smooth sailing. Sometimes we will rock the boat. Sometimes we will experience some backlash from others. But often, when we do, it is for one of two reasons:

- Because they have become familiar and comfortable with the past version of you
- It triggers something within themselves because perhaps they are not being true to themselves, and they are projecting that onto you

You have to ask yourself whether you would prefer to risk confronting these situations in the pursuit of connecting to your authentic self, or risk living a life that is unauthentic. If you choose the latter, it will ultimately lead to resentment, disappointment and regret. And that is not a risk worth taking. Because you deserve to be the fullest and most authentic expression of yourself. Why would you want to be a cookie-cutter version of somebody else?

It is somewhat normal for us to want to be surrounded by like-minded people, and wanting to be accepted by our tribe is a survival mechanism. But our world is different now. It is safe for you to authentically express yourself. And in fact, it is your birthright to do so.

SOUL REFLECTION QUESTIONS

- Why am I bothered by what people think of me?
- Where in my life do I feel pressured to be someone I don't want to be or do something I don't want to do?
- Who would I be if I released all that I felt was expected of me?

Letting go of the good girl and people pleasing

Hands up who resonates with the term 'the good girl'? What about being a people pleaser? These two things can be crippling for your authentic expression, alignment and energetic integrity.

As an example, the story I shared about not drinking or taking drugs theoretically places me in the good girl category, however that *is* an authentic expression for me. If another adult were avoiding alcohol and drugs in order to fit the good girl persona, but felt this persona did not reflect who they wanted to be or how they wanted to behave, that would be an inauthentic expression and suppression of their true self.

The good girl

The good girl archetype can show up in many ways. Maybe growing up you felt you needed to meet an expectation that was placed on you by your parents. Maybe you are 'the nice one' in your group of friends. The one that doesn't have an opinion of their own. The one that sits on the fence for fear of upsetting anyone by expressing their truth or opinion. Maybe you have previously attempted to express your opinion and it was met with ridicule, or you were immediately shut down.

All of these instances, which perhaps at the time don't seem all that significant, remain stored in our subconscious mind. Even if we are not consciously aware of it, when we find ourselves in a similar situation, we may automatically close ourselves off because when we tried to express our truth previously, we were shut down.

When we play the role of the good girl to appease our friends, family or partner, we are not living in truth. We are placing shackles around our soul and it becomes tied to something that is not even ours.

You will be doing yourself and your counterparts a disservice should you continue to play your role as the good girl.

It becomes very difficult to build authentic relationships when you are constantly playing a role, as essentially it is not even the real you people form a connection with. Not to mention how exhausting and unsustainable it is to be a role-player.

If we bring our awareness to and recognise where we are playing out the good girl archetype, we have a much greater chance of releasing these behaviours and taking action that is more authentically aligned for us.

SOUL REFLECTION QUESTIONS

- Where in my life am I playing the role of the good girl?
- What actions do I need to take to release the good girl?

People pleasing

Many of us can resonate with being a people pleaser. It is almost seen as an honourable thing to consistently place others' needs above our own. Why do we do this?

In our society it is seen as selfish to honour yourself first before others. And of course I am not advocating that you go out and move through your life behaving in a selfish manner while not considering others, not at all. It is extremely important to be kind, considerate and compassionate towards others.

What I am suggesting though is that we stop consistently placing others' needs above our own, and that we stop trying to please everyone (which is a futile pursuit by the way!) because of our need for external validation.

Here are a few reasons I believe so many of us are people pleasing.

Guilt

When somebody asks us to do something for them, we feel guilty if we say no. Despite the fact that we may not have the time, resources or energetic capacity to help them, we say yes anyway.

Similarly, if we are invited to an event that we do not want to attend, we feel too guilty or think we will appear flakey if we say no. So we drag ourselves there anyway to appease the person who invited us, despite the fact we would have much preferred to decline the invitation.

Lack of self-esteem/self-worth

We use people pleasing as a tool to compensate for our lack of self-worth. If we are not feeling intrinsically worthy, we might look to source a sense of worth outside of ourselves.

If we are known as the selfless one, the one who is always helping everybody else out, then we receive praise from others, which allows us to cultivate a sense of worthiness externally (rather than internally). We become attached to this notion; it begins to form a part of our identity and we are not sure who we are without it.

We will explore self-worth in greater detail in the next chapter.

Habit

Similar to the previous point, if we have been a long-term people pleaser, it will have become a part of our identity and we will perpetuate these behaviours simply out of habit. It's what we are used to and feel comfortable with.

Just like any other habit that we wish to break, it will take time, commitment and persistence to change.

What we need to recognise is that—similar to the good girl role—people pleasing is unsustainable and will deplete your energetic field. *You need to serve yourself before serving others.* It is impossible to continue pleasing and serving others if you are not allowing yourself to receive, and not nourishing and looking after yourself first.

I am certainly not suggesting that you shy away from serving others. Quite the opposite actually. The service of others can cultivate a deep sense of connection and reverence. However, it needs to come from a genuine place. There needs to be a sense of reciprocity, both giving and receiving. And it needs to come from a place where you are so internally filled up that you are overflowing and able to serve from that place. Otherwise, you will eventually run yourself into the ground energetically, and feel disconnected from yourself and others.

SOUL REFLECTION
QUESTIONS

- Where in my life am I people pleasing?
- In what ways can I serve myself first?
- In what ways do I feel I am being genuinely in service in my life?
- In what ways am I being in service because of a feeling of obligation or a desire to fill a void within myself?

Once you have identified any areas or situations in your life where you are people pleasing, you will become really clear and honest with yourself about where you are acting from a genuine place of being in service, and where you are coming from a place of lack within yourself.

If you are used to operating from a place of lack, it will likely take some time and compassion for yourself to break the cycle. But you are taking the first step by bringing awareness to it. You can utilise practices such as creating boundaries and protecting your energy to support you in this, and we are going to explore this in the next chapter, so sit tight!

Connect to your inner wild woman

There are many different characters in the world of archetypes, but the one that stuck with me was the wild woman. To me, the wild woman represents being untethered, boundless, limitless, raw, real and vulnerable. She is deeply connected to nature and all that surrounds her, and most importantly is connected to her true self.

The wild woman has no expectations of herself or others. She is not concerned about what people think of her. She remains wild and free. She is the embodiment of her true essence. She performs sacred rituals that support her, and she takes care of herself first and foremost so that she can serve herself and others. She can't be tamed. She does not conform to what is outside of herself, and she is deeply guided by her intuition.

Now that we are unshackling ourselves from playing the good girl and people pleasing, I invite you to step into your inner wild woman. This will really allow you to be honest with yourself, set the foundations to connect to your true self, bring things back to basics, and let your soul roam free.

Take some time to sit with and contemplate what the wild woman means to you. And if there is some level of resistance arising for you around embodying this way of being, know that there is medicine in it for you. In what ways can you allow yourself to be untamed, wild, a free spirit?

EXERCISE

Identify some ways to connect to your inner wild woman on a regular basis. Get to know her, and bring her out as often as you feel called to.

Walk your own path

Have you ever felt that you were pursuing something because someone told you to, or you saw somebody else doing it, or you thought that's what you were 'supposed' to do? Maybe you are in that place as you read these words. I feel we are particularly susceptible to this when we have not yet cultivated a deep connection to ourselves and a deep sense of self-awareness.

It can be scary to feel that you haven't got a clear direction because you haven't yet accessed your internal compass, aka your intuition (we are going to explore intuition very soon!). This is when we might start to look around us at what other people are doing to try to gain some bearings on where we are heading in our own life. You might see someone becoming really 'successful' in their career or personal life and have the belief that if you emulate their actions, this will become true for you too.

But it doesn't work this way.

If you are always looking around at what everyone else is doing, rather than looking within, you will never know what is true for you. It will only lead to you comparing yourself to others and potentially wandering onto a path that is not right for you.

It is so important that we don't allow ourselves to feel pressured to be like somebody else, do what somebody else is doing, or simply just do what somebody tells us to do. Just because something is normal or accepted, doesn't make it the right action for us. This is where you need to use your discernment and tune into your intuition to decide what the best action is for you.

I can relate to this situation in my own life. When I first stepped into my own business, it was all so foreign to me. I wasn't sure how I was supposed to act, what offerings I should provide or how to price my services. I looked to others who were in a similar field to see how they ran their business, and I attempted to emulate some of their ways. But as I came to discover, what works for *them* won't necessarily work for *me*. When I tuned into what it was that I really wanted to offer, and how I wanted to run my business according to my unique makeup, things began to flow and feel easeful, rather than difficult.

We have no idea what is going on behind closed doors for others in their life or business. We don't know their background, their energetic makeup, whether or not they have staff or contractors assisting them.

Your path has to feel true for you. It has to feel in alignment with your values and your goals. We can use others for inspiration and guidance, but in the end we are the only one who knows what is true for us.

Do not attempt to walk somebody else's path. There is a path that is a perfect fit for you: you just have to take the first step.

On the flip side to this, I have had some amazing teachers and mentors along the way that have guided and taught me while I found my grounding in my own authenticity. A teacher or guide is ultimately there to support you to connect to your true essence and find the answers within.

Alongside our unique energetic makeup, we also have what is known as dharma, which is our life purpose. At the end of this book, once you have cultivated a deep connection to your authentic self, you are going to explore dharma so that you can form an understanding of what your life's purpose is.

The ultimate takeaway here is to be true to you. Be both inspired and inspiring!

SOUL REFLECTION QUESTIONS

- Where have I been walking somebody else's path?
- What does the path that I desire to walk on look like?
- What are my deepest dreams and desires? (I invite you to discard any preconceived notions you have around whether your dreams and desires are 'achievable' or not. Nothing is off limits, and this will help you later on when we dive into your dharma.)

CHAPTER 3

Know that you are worthy

Owning our worthiness is an act of
acknowledging that we are sacred.

Brené Brown

Detaching yourself from limiting beliefs

How many times have you doubted yourself, thought *People like me don't do things like that* or *I just come from a normal family and so this particular thing isn't available to me,* or deduced yourself to 'living a normal life' when really you wanted to reach for the stars? Some of these limiting thoughts might sound familiar to you; I know they do to me.

These limiting thoughts, and many more, were running

through my mind for so many years. When you are in them, they seem real. They seem true, like they are the only reality that is available for you. And it's not until you have some kind of awakening experience that you begin to see these thoughts for what they really are. You see that these thoughts are, in fact, not true. What you are really telling yourself is that you are not worthy of all that you desire. And that is also not the truth.

Remember my story from the beginning of the book about my airline job that was no longer aligned and becoming toxic? Alongside this, I also worked part-time at a natural therapies clinic with which I had the same experience. In the beginning I really enjoyed it, but the longer I stayed the less aligned it became, and the more entangled my identity became in it. I will always be so grateful for all that I learnt about herbal medicine and natural therapies while I was in the position, but I always held the desire for something more. I was also half-heartedly and not so successfully trying to pursue my own business on the side, which of course did not succeed because I didn't believe that I was worthy, and my energy was scattered all over the place.

I found myself bouncing back and forth between these two jobs, hoping to gain a different experience from the same situations. I was running around here, there and everywhere just trying to earn a living and maintain the facade of who others perceived me to be and the self-image I was attempting to uphold. And the reason I did this was because it was familiar, it was comfortable, it was known to me.

It is not comfortable or easy when we step outside our comfort zone, and I wasn't prepared to do that for quite some time. So I stayed in this cycle until I had learnt the lessons that I needed to.

One day I finally had this awakening within me that more was in store for me, and I was worthy and capable of holding it.

I think there were multiple reasons why I allowed myself to be swallowed up by my limiting beliefs for so long. Some of these included toxic relationships and working environments, not really knowing exactly what work I wanted to do in the world, and most prominently being disconnected from my true self, my true authentic essence. All of this led me to feeling lost and confused about who I was, and what my purpose was in this lifetime.

Throughout my twenties I did discover my passion for wellness, and that has evolved and changed many times since then, and will continue to do so into the future. In my own wellness practices and experiences, I began to discover parts of who I was and who I desired to be. This path began with focusing on physical fitness and nutrition. I worked out at the gym five or six days a week and ensured that I was eating nutritious foods. This really was the gateway for me to begin exploring what it means to be well, and it served its purpose at the time.

I began to think that this was something I could explore as a career option and it led me to studying to become a personal trainer. But during this process I discovered yoga, and this caused a big shift that changed the course of my life. The more I began to explore yoga, the less interested

I was in just focusing on fitness and nutrition, and I fell headfirst onto the yogic path. I will share in greater detail the impact that my yoga practice has had on me in Chapter 5, and how it served as a valuable lesson.

Maybe you have had a similar experience in your own life? Where one day you suddenly realise that there is another way, that you are capable of anything that you desire, and that there is something more out there for you. Maybe you are having this experience right now as you read the pages of this book.

Why do we limit ourselves?

We as humans have infinite potential. We are boundless. So why do we place limitations on ourselves? Why do we keep ourselves small, when we really want to soar? Why do we dull our sparkle when all we want to do is shine?

We get comfortable where we are and become afraid to explore anything outside of our comfort zone. We make excuses, we self-sabotage, we turn down opportunities that could potentially lead us forward along our journey. There are many reasons why we may place limitations on ourselves, including societal conditioning, past trauma or wounding, or limiting beliefs that are planted in our subconscious mind.

We can get so caught up in our 'story' about what has been true for us so far in our life that it becomes a part of our perceived identity, and we don't know who we are without it. We get comfortable and familiar with playing the victim and suffering due to our circumstances, but for whatever reason we aren't able to make a change and break free of the shackles we have placed on ourselves. We become too afraid to remove the armour that we have spent so long accumulating to hide ourselves, to protect ourselves. Afraid that if we remove the armour we will become vulnerable, or be seen for our true selves; when you conjure up the courage to take off the amour, there is always the risk of perceived rejection and non-acceptance from others.

But you need to ask yourself, do you want to spend your life pretending to be something that you are not, never reaching your fullest potential? Or would you rather remove your amour, shine your light and step into the highest version of yourself, knowing that there is a small risk you might not be accepted by others? Do you want to look back on your life knowing that you explored every opportunity and every desire that was in your heart? Or that you didn't even give yourself the opportunity to do so? The choice is yours. There are endless opportunities available to you, all you need to do is be brave enough to reach out and take a hold of them.

Often it can take some time for us to identify limiting patterns that we are repeating in our life. Sometimes a significant event unfolds that acts as a catalyst for change. Sometimes it's a progressive unfolding over time as we work on ourselves and begin to uncover who we are. It could be that one day you just wake up, decide that you are tired of the old patterns playing out in your life, and realise you are worthy of more.

It is important to note that more often than not we

are unaware of the limiting beliefs that we carry in our subconscious mind, and this is where it can be of great benefit to work with a practitioner who can assist you in identifying and releasing these patterns.

I recently went through The Spiral journey with my kinesiologist Zoe Bosco. We unlocked a lot of limiting beliefs that had been buried in my subconscious mind, holding me back from the life that I desired. What we don't realise is that events that took place in our childhood, and sometimes while we were still in the womb, can anchor emotions and limiting beliefs into our subconscious mind and get entangled in our physical and energetic bodies.

A seemingly small event that takes place while you are a small child can trigger a negative emotion and a limiting belief in your mind and body. This is why it can be so beneficial to work with a practitioner who can help you identify and release these limiting beliefs and patterns so you are free to step into your highest self.

Know this—if you are currently being held back by limiting beliefs or replaying the same negative patterns in your life right now, it does not have to stay this way. You can unshackle yourself from your perceived limitations, from your fears, from anything that has been holding you back for so long. Because you deserve to live the life that you desire.

Releasing limiting beliefs

What beliefs do you hold about yourself that are limiting your potential? I bet a few come to mind in an instant. How many of those beliefs are actually based on truth? Probably not many. Most of us are forecasting into the future, running potential scenarios through our mind that are unlikely to come to fruition at all, and yet we allow these thoughts to overrun us, causing anxiety and overwhelm.

Limiting beliefs are common amongst many of us. And they can become crippling. They can paralyse us, make us hesitant to move for fear of what might happen, how we might be judged by others, how we might 'fail'. Unless we make the conscious decision to unravel them, they will prevent us from pursuing the things that we desire. And not only that: if we consistently run the same negative thought patterns through our mind, negativity is what we will keep on attracting, because we create our own reality. We will explore this concept later in the book.

Cast your mind back to the moment you began to mistakenly believe that you were not worthy of that which you desired. Perhaps it was during your childhood, your turbulent teenage years, or your early twenties when you were dealing with relationships, navigating your career and embracing womanhood. What was it that triggered this response and this belief about yourself? There could be more than one answer. Hold them in your awareness now.

Holding these moments in your awareness, find a comfortable seat and gently close your eyes. Feel and see these moments now for a minute or two. Recognise how they feel for you, and how they may arise in your life. Then set the intention to consciously let them go. Make the decision that they are not based in truth, and you no longer wish to carry them with you anymore. Visualise and feel these situations that have interfered with your self-worth melting away from your mind, body and soul.

Notice how you feel in your body and your energy. Do you feel lighter? More open and receptive?

Leaning into self-worth

On a scale of one to ten, how worthy do you feel at present? Be honest with yourself here. There's no judgement; you are simply creating awareness. Once you are aware of something, you can then make decisions about how to address it.

Write the number down in your journal.

Now consider the way that you speak to yourself: your internal dialogue. Is it kind, compassionate, understanding, nurturing and supportive? Or do you criticise yourself, talk down to yourself, or tell yourself you are not good enough?

What we say and think about ourselves matters, *a lot.* Whether you are saying aloud things that are unkind about yourself, in a joking fashion or not, or thinking unkind things in your mind, these words are all being reinforced in your mind and being. On the flip side, can you recall times where you felt really confident in yourself and overflowing with self-worth? You may recall only a few, or perhaps many. Either way, I want you to anchor into how it felt when you were feeling confident and worthy within yourself. What was going on for you in those moments? Was there a commonality between them?

It is a common experience for people to endure things that they really shouldn't have to because their sense of self-worth is low. Perhaps you can relate to this in your past or current life? I have been in situations in workplaces, friendships and relationships where I have tolerated behaviours and been treated poorly because at the time my self-worth was low and I had not yet formed a deep connection to myself. I had not yet had the awakening I needed to realise and own my worthiness. It's not until you begin to do this deep inner work, connect deeply to your true self and own your worth that you can form a clear understanding of what you will or will not accept and enforce this lovingly.

To use my job at the airline again as an example, it took a long series of events for me to finally come to the realisation that I would no longer tolerate being undermined in my knowledge and my capabilities, and that I no longer wanted somebody other than myself dictating my worth via a modest hourly wage. This notion can also present itself in other situations such as romantic relationships, friendships and family dynamics.

———————   E X E R C I S E   ———————

Take a moment to pause here again and close your eyes. Begin to tune into the feeling of self-worth. Notice how it feels in your physical body, mind, and soul. It might not necessarily feel comfortable for you, particularly if you are not used to feeling a sense of worthiness. Become curious here—lean all the way into it. Stay here in this feeling as long as it takes for you to become comfortable and familiar with it. Allow this feeling of deep self-worth to permeate your being so it is all that you know.

Now that you are familiar with the feeling of self-worth, it is time to embody this way of being. You set the standard for how you feel about yourself, for how others treat you and what you will or will not accept. You are a divine feminine being who is here on the earth to shine brightly, to embody your true way of being, to reach your highest potential. And by doing so, you inspire others to do the same.

Do not settle for less than what you deserve. Know that you are worthy. Feel it in the very essence of your being. Own it, you deserve it all!

SOUL REFLECTION
QUESTIONS

- Where am I currently allowing behaviours to occur that I deem inappropriate?
- What am I currently accepting that is less than the threshold of what I deserve?
- What changes do I need to make so that I can fully own my worth?
- What practices can I participate in to support my worthiness?
- What limiting self-beliefs do I need to release to raise my self-worth?

Solar plexus meditation

The solar plexus chakra (Manipura), located in the centre of the stomach, is represented by the colour yellow and is the home of our self-worth. This is our power centre. It is from this place that we are able to shine brightly and embrace our true essence.

A solar plexus that is underactive or holding stagnant or blocked energy can lead to us not embodying our power. We may feel shy in expressing our power, and we may lack confidence and self-worth.

Find a comfortable seated position and close your eyes. Sit with a straight spine, relax your shoulders and jaw, and connect to your natural breath. Bring your awareness to your solar plexus chakra, right in the centre of your stomach. Notice how your solar plexus currently feels energetically and physically. Now visualise a bright yellow light shining brightly. Visualise this bright yellow light illuminating the path you are about to walk on. Begin to tune deeply into the energy of your solar plexus. Connect to the power that is available to you in this energy centre. Anchor the feeling of your internal power that is available to you always, knowing that it is there for you to access at all times. Stay here for as long as you need to to form a deep connection to your power and worthiness.

Other ways to support your solar plexus

You can support your solar plexus with yellow crystals such as citrine, twisting yoga poses, and by basking in the sunlight.

Tuning into your intuition, aka your internal compass

Women are by nature extremely intuitive. However, it is common for us to become disconnected from ourselves and our intuition as we become more connected to things such as modern technology and keeping ourselves perpetually 'busy'. We all have access to our intuition at all times. It is our internal compass that gently guides us in the right direction. And if you tune into and trust in your intuition, you are unlikely to be led astray.

How can we begin to tune into and trust in our intuition?

We need to create space to hear our intuition by quieting the external noise. If we don't make quiet time to tune into ourselves, how will we hear it? How will we be able to differentiate our thoughts from the thoughts of those around us?

Once we have quietened the noise, and connected back to self, we can become acutely aware of how our body responds. You will often experience a physical response in your body when an intuitive message is being transmitted to you. It's that drop or butterflies in your stomach. It's the heat or energy in your body. It's that unexplainable feeling of 'just knowing' when something or some action is right for you or not.

You have likely had an experience in your life at some point—I know that I have—where you have just had a feeling, an inner knowing, about whether to do something or not, and then it ends up being the right course of action for you. Trust in that. Use that as an example to know and trust in your intuition. Even if it doesn't make logical sense. Even if it conflicts with what someone else is telling you. Even if it seems scary or out of your comfort zone.

When we make time to slow down and be still, this is where the magic happens. This is where we can gain guidance from our internal compass. This is when messages will come through that you might have otherwise missed if you were busy being 'busy'.

Trusting your intuition will give you the best chance of leaning into what is right for you and remaining on a path that is true for you.

If we really tune into our intuition in each and every moment, we will discover that all of the answers are already within. And of course there will be times where it will be beneficial to seek the guidance of a mentor or loved one, but ultimately the only one who truly knows what is right for us is ourselves. Connecting to our intuition plays a vital role in connecting to our authentic self.

Make a commitment to yourself to sit in stillness every day so that you can connect to your intuitive wisdom. Let intuition be your guiding light.

A note on self-worth and intuition

When you have raised your self-worth and built confidence and trust in your ability to handle anything in life, you will never question your intuition. Rather than trying to outsource your decision making to someone that is outside of yourself, you can look within and know that you hold all of the guidance you need.

Self-worth and intuition are intertwined, and this is one of the reasons it is so important to understand and embody your worthiness so that you can have faith in the guidance that is shown to you through your intuition.

Connecting to your intuition through your Ajna chakra

Our third-eye chakra (Ajna) is the home of our intuition. The third eye is located between the eyebrows and is represented by the colour indigo. Our third eye can often show us things that our physical eyes are blind to. It can show us a higher or different perspective on situations.

If you have felt challenged when trying to connect to your intuition, I encourage you to form a deep connection to your third eye, either through your own practice or by using the following third-eye meditation.

Third-eye meditation

Take a comfortable seat with the spine long, even weight between your sit bones, and the shoulders, neck and jaw relaxed. Take a moment to still your mind and body, and connect deeply to your breath. Just notice your breath moving in and out through your nostrils.

Now bring your awareness to your third eye, and become familiar with it. Connect energetically to the third eye, feel the energy in this space.

Now visualise an indigo-coloured orb of light at your third eye. Keeping your eyes closed, direct your gaze upwards towards your third eye. Take a look inside. Notice what you feel. Notice any images, symbols or colours that come to you when you gaze to your third eye.

Now begin to expand your gaze out even wider, and allow your third eye to show you the bigger picture, a higher or different perspective. Stay here as long as you need to.

When you feel called to, begin to narrow your focus and bring your awareness and your gaze back to your third eye, and then gently release the gaze and open your eyes.

Remain deeply connected to what you saw through your third eye. You might like to write down in your journal anything that you were shown or any wisdom that was imparted to you during your third-eye meditation.

SOUL REFLECTION QUESTIONS

- When I slow down and connect to my intuition, what does it try to tell me?
- What do I already intuitively know I need to do that I have been ignoring or suppressing?
- When I close my eyes and turn my gaze towards my third eye, what can I see? (e.g. patterns, colours, images, forecasts/ premonitions)
- What can I see when I look at things from a higher perspective?

Become a joy seeker

Joy is one of the highest vibrational frequencies for us to reside in, so it's understandable that we want to seek more joy in our lives. I think it is pretty safe to say that the vast majority of us are not residing in joy the majority of the time. We allow external situations to alter our internal state of being. We feel stressed, worried, anxious. We do things that we don't actually want to do and that do not bring us joy. And we are so used to operating in this way that we probably don't remember what real joy actually feels like.

When we are experiencing a low sense of self-worth, we feel that we are not deserving of joy, and we settle for less than we desire and deserve. Can you see how your level of self-worth influences the level of joy that you experience in your life?

Take a moment to reflect on what brings you joy, and I mean real joy. Write it down in your journal.

Now write down the things that aren't bringing you joy in your life right now. Remember, we can still love and be grateful for these things, while also acknowledging that they aren't bringing us joy. The first step to making a shift is to acknowledge them.

Now that you have a list of what brings you joy and what doesn't, write down some ways that you can incorporate more of the things that bring you joy into your everyday life. Aspire to do at least one thing each day that brings joy to your life. Look at where you can make time in your day to prioritise joy.

Take a look again at your list of things that aren't joyful in your life, and ask yourself these questions:

- If these things aren't bringing me joy, why am I doing them?
- Why am I holding on to these things? Is there an underlying reason behind it?

Don't waste another minute of your precious life doing something that doesn't light you up. It will only deplete your energy and rob you of those precious moments of joy that are available to you.

Take some time now to think about and write down ways that you can:

- Swap out something that is not joyful for something that is

- Find joy in the things that currently aren't bringing you joy
- Remove things that aren't joyful from your life

If there is a task in your business or life that you do not enjoy, look at ways that you can outsource this to someone who specialises in that task.

If you are currently in a situation that you do not enjoy (e.g. a job or relationship), write down some steps that you can take to either make the situation more joyful, if that is an option, or move out of the situation.

We want to be realistic with the time that we have available to us each day, but also ensure that we commit to, and see the value in, finding joy.

Try this joy-seeking experiment out and observe how it impacts you. Notice if there is any change in your mood, your happiness, or your life generally.

Now you will have a good understanding of what brings you joy and what doesn't, and some tangible steps that you can take to bring you closer to joy in your everyday life.

Connecting to joy through the heart charka

If you struggle to connect with the emotion of joy or identify what truly brings you joy, I encourage you to drop into your heart and connect to your heart chakra (Anahata).

The heart chakra is located right near the sternum and is represented by the colour green. It is the hub of love, joy and compassion, and this is a beautiful place to really feel that deep sense of joy.

The heart chakra is arguably the most important of our seven main chakras as it is the bridge between our earthly selves (lower three chakras) and our highest selves (higher three chakras).

Heart chakra meditation

Close your eyes and begin to energetically connect to your heart chakra. Feel the vibration of it in your chest. Now visualise a green orb of light at the centre of your heart. Visualise an open channel of energy moving inward and outward from your heart centre. Allow yourself to fully receive as much love and joy as you give.

Now allow your heart to lead the way as you start to visualise and connect to the feeling of joy, and notice what arises for you when you do this. Maybe it's a person, an activity or a place. Notice what naturally sparks a feeling of joy within you. Really feel a deep sense of love, joy, compassion and connection to yourself and all that is.

Stay in this place of joy as long as you can. Once you begin to come out of your meditative state, keep that connection to your heart centre and the feelings of joy.

You might feel called to write down in your journal all of the things that aligned with you when you embodied the feeling of joy. Then you can return to this list, and return to the heart meditation, anytime you want to be reminded of your feelings of joy.

Creating loving boundaries and protecting your energy

What are energetic boundaries?

In a nutshell, they are energy shields that we can put in place to ensure we are not taking on energy or 'stuff' that is not ours. It is vital that we put these boundaries in place to prevent our energy from becoming depleted and tainted by taking on energy that is not ours.

Also, every encounter throughout our day can see us leave parts of our energy behind, and we want to have the awareness and ability to draw our energy back to us.

I found myself in a situation with a close friend where there was a large imbalance in the exchange of energy, and a lack of reciprocity. Over time, I began to realise that my friend would only reach out when they needed something from me, such as advice, or when they needed to off-load all of their issues onto me. And although there were some positive things that remained within the friendship, ultimately I realised that the bad was outweighing the good, and it was causing me to feel stressed, upset and energetically drained.

Even though it was challenging, I expressed all of these thoughts and feelings to this friend, and our friendship ended up dissolving. It was upsetting and took some adjusting, but this is an example of how I needed to put a strong boundary in place in order to protect myself, my energy and my integrity.

Maybe you have had a similar experience in your life where you have felt taken advantage of, or where there has been an imbalance in a relationship.

These practices will look different for all of us, but I will share a few examples of where your energy could be depleted and ways you can implement boundaries to protect your energy.

Just noting here that we can also put boundaries in place for ourselves, not just when we are interacting with others. Some situations where you could find yourself taking on other people's energy include:

In crowded public places

If you, like me, are sensitive to other people's energies, you might not particularly enjoy being in crowded public places. For me, it does depend on how I am feeling on any given day—sometimes I find it quite ok—but I'd say for the most part I feel quite uncomfortable and even slightly anxious going to public places.

Places such as shopping centres are so far removed from the kind of natural environment that we should be habituating—with the fluoro lights, linear aisles, freezing cold air with no ventilation, blazing sounds and music.

Some ways that I make my trip to the shops a little more pleasant are:

- Going outside of peak times
- Focusing on my breath
- Being intentional while I'm there: not getting distracted buying things I don't need and making my stay longer than it has to be

- Wearing crystals (clear quartz is great) to protect my energy from other energies around me
- Avoiding the shopping centre where possible and instead choosing the organic store and farmers' market (it is so much better for your health)

You can also put on your energetic shield with the intention of keeping yourself energetically safe and secure. Set an intention of not allowing other people's energy to penetrate your energetic field, and not allowing others to draw from your energy field.

There are times when we have to go to the shopping centre or airport but don't particularly want to be in that environment. Having these tools available to us can help us feel much better equipped when we do.

When a friend is off-loading their problems onto you

I think it's safe to say that we have all experienced at one time or another a friend, a family member or even a work colleague persistently complaining or off-loading their issues and problems onto us.

And yes, we absolutely should be there for our loved ones when they need us. But relationships, no matter what kind, are a two-way street. There needs to be an equal energy exchange, otherwise there will be an imbalance in the relationship. If one person is always giving and one person is always taking, over time this will lead to resentment and energetic depletion in the one who is always giving.

Some tips I have around navigating this are:

For friendships, family and relationships

- Engage with them when you have the full capacity to hold space for them.
- Aim for open and honest communication. They are not mind-readers. Let them know how you are feeling.
- Let them know that you would really appreciate reciprocity in your relationship.
- Create some space—take some time out from the situation and gain some perspective.

If after moving through all of these steps the situation doesn't improve, maybe you need to move on from the relationship or friendship, or spend less time with that family member.

In your work environment

If you have ever worked within a team, you would likely have experienced a team member who was oozing with negative vibes. It is not a nice feeling and can change the energy of the whole room, and the whole work environment.

My suggestion is to not engage with this energy. You can be polite and friendly, but there is no need to be overly involved.

Similarly, if you have a colleague that off-loads their

issues onto you, you can take similar steps to the ones mentioned for family and friends and communicate honestly about how you're feeling. Let them know you'd appreciate a fairer energy exchange in your working relationship.

Remember that you do not owe anything to anyone. You are not obliged to engage in gossiping or fix other people's problems.

When working with clients

When working one-on-one with clients, there are a few things that I would suggest to protect your energy:

- Make sure that both parties are clear on the intention and expectations of the other party. Your client knows exactly what the service is that you are going to provide and what is included in that, and likewise you have stated what commitment you expect from your client. This might include a contract stating the specifics of the agreement.
- Put boundaries in place around when clients can contact you and via what channel, and what your response time will be; make it clear when you are available and when you are not.
- Maintain the integrity of the client/practitioner relationship and what that entails. Avoid stepping outside of that or creating blurry lines around what that looks like.

When communicating with people

Any interaction with another person—whether face to face, over the phone or online—has the potential to impact your energy field. Generally, I recommend:

- Not giving away all of your knowledge through free advice. Your time, knowledge and skills are valuable and it is not an equal energy exchange if you are giving your services away for free regularly.
- Placing boundaries for yourself around when you will engage with social media.
- Not making yourself overly available to people. Remember that every interaction takes a piece of our energy, and this includes online interactions. This means getting back to people when you can and not feeling obliged to drop everything and reply or engage straight away.
- Only engaging with social media when you have the capacity. Don't spend all day mindlessly on social media. It is so detrimental for us, and for what? Make it an intentional activity to check your socials during an allocated time period and then move on.

Some other ways that we can protect our energy that I haven't yet mentioned are:

- Using tools such as crystals, sage and essential

oil sprays to clear the energy that may have been transferred to you

- Calling on angels or guides to protect you
- Using meditation with the intention of drawing your energy back

Remember that your energy is your highest priority. It's your most valuable currency. It is everything. And sometimes in order to protect our energy, we do need to put ourselves and our energetic needs first. That may mean enforcing some boundaries or saying no to things, and this might make you feel uncomfortable at first. But over time, you will grow more comfortable with this and recognise its value. And when we can protect and nurture our energy, we are supported to always be connected to our true self; we are supported to live the life that we desire, and be well and happy. And there will be more of us to share with the world.

Part II

CHAPTER 4

The dance between masculine and feminine energy

The union of feminine and masculine energies within an individual is the basis of all creation.

Shakti Gawain

You might have heard the terms masculine and feminine energy thrown around a lot lately, but what do they actually mean? We all have both energies within us always, but getting the balance between the two is sometimes easier said than done.

There have been times where I have been a lot more in one energy than the other, causing me to be out of balance in my energy. Take the example of me working all of those jobs at the same time, hustling, running around, living the grind-to-five life. This looked like waking up early so that I could squeeze in some kind of morning routine, getting ready and heading to one job, then changing uniforms and heading to the other job, then teaching a yoga class, fitting in my daily walk (my walks are what keep me sane!), having dinner and going to bed, all to do it again the following day. That is a classic example of being way too far in your masculine energy. The rushing around, the pushing, the lack of presence, the 'go go go, do do do' mentality is a classic one-way ticket to adrenal fatigue or complete burnout.

On the other hand, there have been times more recently where there has been too much flow, lack of direction, and not enough structure in my life. And to be honest, it was probably because I had been so far in my masculine that once I had the opportunity to, I went completely in the opposite direction and embraced the feminine energy. This for me looked like waking up without an alarm, slow mornings, getting to my desk late and not having any structure or guidance around what I wanted to achieve for the day. While it is a nice opportunity to have that freedom and flexibility, it is not always conducive to productivity and staying on course in the direction you want to go. There is no real fire. There is no real passion or fuelled action. There is no clear direction or road map of where you want to go when you are operating in this way.

Personally, leaning into the feminine has allowed me to:

- Be more balanced with my energy and in my life

as a whole
- Gain better health through making space for nurturing rituals and prioritising my health
- Understand myself at a deeper level, again because I now make the time and space to know myself better

How to identify and work with each energy

So what exactly are the masculine and feminine energies? And how can we use these energies to our advantage? How can we live in flow and alignment with these energies?

Let's explore this!

Masculine energy

Before we begin, let's get something straight. When you envision masculine energy, it is not a burly muscular man using his physical energy and strength to get things done (although there might be times when that is useful!).

The masculine energy within us all represents taking action, structure, and that internal fire and drive. When you operate too far in (or too often from) your masculine energy, you risk losing those precious moments of connecting to your intuition, being present and just generally enjoying each moment. When you are always pushing and doing, you also risk throwing yourself way out of balance, and this could lead to complete burnout.

And when that happens, you will have no choice but to completely surrender and lean more into the feminine energy.

When you can take a more balanced approach to the feminine and masculine energies, you are far less likely to become unbalanced and depleted.

And although most of us have been running too much from our masculine, you can see that these qualities are imperative for taking aligned action and actually getting the thing done!

Don't be afraid to really embody masculine energy when you need to, rather than fearing burnout. Just become really aware of which energy you are in at any given moment. This may take some getting used to, but again it comes back to becoming really self-aware and knowing how each energy works best for you!

Some ways that you can lean more into masculine energy include:

Making lists

Lists help us know exactly what actions we need to take and what we need to get done. There is nothing more satisfying than crossing things off a to-do list!

Structuring your life

Using a calendar to organise your day can help ensure that you allow adequate time for everything you need to get done each day or week. And this also includes time for taking care of yourself with exercise, fun activities or dedicated rest time.

Taking aligned action towards your goals

You can dream about what it is that you want to achieve, but if you are not taking *action* towards it, it will not happen, or it will take a lot longer to happen! If you have a big goal that you'd like to achieve and it seems a little overwhelming, break it down into smaller actionable steps that you can take each week or month.

Getting passionate about what lights you up

If you are not passionate about what you are doing, continuing down this path will not be sustainable or enjoyable. You need to feel excited and passionate about what you are doing! You need that fire in your belly to keep you going when times get tough or things are taking longer than you expected.

Going after what you desire

Know that you are capable and deserving of what you desire. Set your eye on the prize, leave some wriggle room for the Universe to work its magic, and then go for it! Use your passion to propel you forward towards your goal.

SOUL REFLECTION QUESTIONS

- How can I tap into my masculine energy?
- Do I need more structure in my life to support my goals and desires?
- Where do I need to take more action in my life?

Feminine energy

The feminine energy within us is softer. It represents our intuitive nature, flow and ease, receptivity, creativity, and really connecting with how things make us *feel*.

In order to really embody these qualities, you need to create space to tune into them.

The feminine energy does not rush. She does not play into the ego. She is not afraid to ask for help when she needs it. Leaning into our feminine energy gives us life. The divine feminine *is* the giver of life. She allows us to become a creative channel and find restoration at a deep level. Most importantly, she supports us to connect with our intuition and our higher self.

And when we are tuning into ourselves, we discover that we always have the answers we need within. We know what the next step is by feeling into it, rather than thinking.

Residing too much in our feminine can also become detrimental, just as being too much in our masculine can. When we spend too much time in feminine energy, we may become stagnant, we may not take any action, or we may be too much in flow to commit to anything. It really is a dance between the two energies and finding a beautiful balance, which will look different for each of us.

Some ways that you can connect with your feminine energy include:

Tapping into your creativity

Whichever creative pursuits light you up and allow you to feel inspired and in a flow state, make time to prioritise them in your life. This is really going to support you to lean into your feminine energy.

Become aligned with your intuition

Align with your intuition by creating space to hear it and by trusting it *no matter what.*

Taking time alone to tune into your intuition is going to serve you immensely. Feminine energy is very intuitive and this is a great way for you to lean into this energy and trust your innate wisdom.

Create more ease and flow in your life

Have you been doing things the hard way? Are there some ways that you could streamline your life to help you lean into your feminine energy with more ease and grace?

If something feels hard or out of alignment, look at some ways that you can create more ease, or perhaps you need to release it. Use your intuition to guide you.

Make decisions by how things make you feel

We hold so much wisdom within ourselves, in our physical, emotional and energetic bodies. And this wisdom is not to be underestimated!

It can be tempting to purely use logic in our decision-making processes. I mean, if it makes logical sense to do something, it must be the right thing, right? Not necessarily. What looks good on paper or makes sense from a logical perspective will not always align with how we intrinsically *feel* about it.

While logic has its place, I invite you to use your intuition and the wisdom of your body next time you need to make some big decisions, and listen to the whispers that are provided to you. This will rarely lead you to an incorrect decision.

Ask for help when you need it

Feminine energy is receptive. She is not afraid to ask for help when she needs it. She gracefully accepts offerings that are presented to her.

Do not feel like you need to go it alone. If someone is offering you assistance that you need, graciously accept it and thank them, knowing that in the spirit of reciprocity you will be more than happy to return the favour in the future should they require it.

EXERCISE

How can you tap into your feminine energy?

Look at how you can implement the techniques we have explored into your life to strengthen your connection with your feminine energy. Perhaps you can do some trial and error and see what works best for you and your unique energy.

The reawakening of divine feminine energy

For what seems like forever, we as citizens of the world have been largely dominated by the masculine energy, particularly in Western cultures. Patriarchal systems have filtered into our schools, workplaces and homes. I have often thought throughout my life, *Who said that things should be this way? Who said we have to do it all with no assistance? Who said that we have to be at work from 9.00 am to 5.00 pm?* Like who was the first person to ever say that was a thing! And somehow it has become cemented into our culture and psyche.

Throughout history we have been sold the idea that women are somehow inferior to men. That we aren't as valuable or worthy. That we aren't deserving of equal pay or opportunity, and that it isn't a priority for us to go after our dreams and desires. We have been encouraged to play small, be submissive, remain suppressed, look pretty and stay quiet.

This paradigm has been passed down through the generations and fostered a warped sense of how a divine feminine being is supposed to live in this existence. This has often led women to become a mere shadow of the fullest expression of ourselves. Imagine a tiny sliver of light trying its hardest to shine through the cracks.

But there is a change sweeping across our planet. We are beginning to see the rise, the reawakening of divine feminine energy. We are beginning to see the crumbling of old rigid systems that are no longer serving humanity. We are seeing injustices and inequalities being brought to light. We are seeing more and more people realising and understanding that there is another way.

When we come to realise that the light is within us, and when we allow it to burst open, it illuminates everything around us. It enables us to step into our fullest potential. It illuminates what was once in the shadows and provides us with a different perspective. It inspires and uplifts those around us and encourages them to let their light shine too.

Can you envision a world where every divine feminine being allowed their light to shine with pride, like the sun shining brightly in the sky? What a different and beautiful experience we would all be having in our world. I believe that this is going to be the future for us; women all over the globe are beginning to reawaken their divine feminine energy and step into their power and their truth.

The crumbling of the old-world ways is not something to be feared, but welcomed, embraced and invited in. For we cannot build something new on an unstable foundation. We cannot build something beautiful on systems that are broken. We need this crumbling to occur. We need the old to fall away, just like the leaves in autumn. We need to release that which is no longer serving us in order to create the space for something new.

This is a time to feel excited! Because we have the opportunity right now to build the world that we desire. A world that is built on love, kindness and compassion. A world full of mutual respect, reciprocity, and creativity.

In this divine future of ours, there will be no need to mask yourself, no fear of speaking up or speaking your truth, no reason to ever feel inferior or submissive. Because you will feel so connected to your authentic self that you will have nothing to fear and nothing to hide. You will become so comfortable in owning your true nature. Not hiding it, not altering it, but fully embodying your true essence.

We can build a world that supports greater freedom, flow and fluidity. A world where people are honoured and celebrated for their authenticity and uniqueness, rather than placed in a box. We can live in a world where women can structure their life and work in a way that is supportive to their menstrual cycle. We can live in a world where we work together to support each other, not compete against each other. For we are one and the same.

This rising of the divine feminine does not in any way detract from the beauty that is within divine masculine energy. However, it does mean that we can begin to release any toxicity and repression that accompanied it. This will lead the way to the feminine and masculine coming together in unison and harmony, with deep love and reverence for one another.

Ask yourself, where can you lean more into this divine feminine energy? What structures are currently in place in your life that are outdated, heavily in the masculine energy, or just no longer serving you?

Metaphysics of masculine and feminine energies

Metaphysics is used to describe the energy and nature of all things. Each part of our physical body represents a particular area in our life. In regards to masculine and feminine energy, the left side of our body represents the feminine, and the right side represents the masculine.

If you can really tune into and become aware of your body, it will communicate to you. It will provide you with signs and signals as to what might be going on in your life. Maybe it starts off with a small whisper that, if ignored, becomes louder and louder and turns into a cry for help.

Let's say that you have a pain in your left hip: the left side is feminine and the hip is a storage area for emotions. This could indicate that you are holding stagnant and stuck energy in your hip due to a feminine energy in your life. This could be a person or a pursuit (such as your creativity), or it could be that you are out of balance in your own feminine energy.

Let's look at another example: say you have a pain in your right knee. The right side is masculine, and the knee represents flexibility in your life. This could indicate that you are being inflexible with a masculine figure in your life, or in your working life.

As you can see, our body is communicating to us all of the time. And if we can take the time to listen, all of the wisdom and guidance that we need will be revealed.

SOUL REFLECTION QUESTIONS

- Have I experienced any aches, pains or niggles on either side of my body that might be communicating with me?
- Have I experienced dis-ease in my body, and if so, where/what was it? What could my body potentially be trying to communicate to me?

Know the nadis

Now I'm going to get a little yoga-nerdy with you here, but further to the masculine and feminine energy discussion, I want to touch on the *ida, pingala* and *sushumna nadis*.

Nadis are energy lines that run throughout our body. The sushumna nadi is the largest energy line in our body, running through the centre of our spinal column. Alongside the sushumna are the ida and pingala nadis. Ida represents feminine energy and is located to the left of the spine, while pingala represents masculine energy and is located to the right. Both the ida and pingala begin at the base of the spine, and coil their way up towards the crown like a serpent.

This is another realm of our subtle energy body that

we can work with to ensure that our energies remain as balanced as possible. One way to do this is to practise *nadi shodhana*, otherwise known as alternate nostril breathing. Throughout the day our breath will fluctuate between entering primarily through the left or right nostril, and when you practise alternate nostril breathing, you will be able to feel that for yourself.

―――――――― E X E R C I S E ――――――――

Alternate nostril breathing

Begin in a comfortable seated position, gently closing your eyes and taking a moment to bring yourself to stillness. Bring your awareness to your natural breath. Bring your index and middle finger to rest at the third eye between the brows. Just become comfortable with having your hand near your face. Curl the ring and pinky fingers in and leave the thumb as it is for now.

Slide the thumb across and block off the left nostril, take a deep inhale through the right nostril, slide the thumb across to block off the right nostril, and exhale through the left nostril. Inhale through left, close off the left and exhale through right.

That is one complete cycle of alternate nostril breathing.

You can continue to do as many rounds as you

like, perhaps starting with five rounds and working your way up to ten or more. Ensure that you complete the cycle by exhaling through the right nostril.

Take a moment of pause at the completion of the practice to observe how you are feeling and any shifts in your energy.

This practice is amazing for balancing your masculine and feminine energies. It is also very calming and cooling for both the physical body and the nervous system.

Bringing the masculine and feminine into divine harmony

If it can be detrimental to be too far in one energy or the other, it makes sense that you would want to find a balance between masculine and feminine energy, right? So how exactly can you do that?

There are a few ways. However, I just want to acknowledge that throughout different times in our lives, we are in fact required to be more in one energy than the other, and that is okay. It is about being aware of when you are in the energy and knowing that it is for a set period of time. Once you have moved through that period of time, you can use the following tools to bring yourself back into balance.

Activities that can support your masculine energy include:

- High-intensity exercise—cardio or weight training
- Yang styles of yoga—hatha, vinyasa, ashtanga
- Potent and detoxifying pranayama practices (not for beginners)—breath of fire or fast rhythmic breathing techniques
- Socialising with friends, family or colleagues— schedule in when you feel like being in the energy of others
- Creating structure in your work life—making lists, following procedures, scheduling
- Taking care of finances and the household to-dos

Activities that can support your feminine energy include:

- Lower-intensity exercise—walking, Pilates, tai chi, qi gong
- Yin yoga and restorative yoga (yin is my fave!)
- Gentle pranayama practices—nadi shodhana or just gentle breathing at a controlled and even pace
- Meditation
- Time for introspection and time alone
- Resting when you need to and completely honouring that—no guilt. Fully surrender to it and embrace the healing qualities that rest brings.
- Getting in touch with your creativity, whatever that looks like for you
- Asking for help from someone if you need it
- Practising more self-care in whatever way resonates with you—massage, taking a bath,

sipping some tea … whatever lights you up!
- Using the sacral chakra meditation in Chapter 8 to connect with your feminine and creative energy on a deeper level

The number-one tip that I can share with you about balancing your energies is to be more self-aware. If you are aware of your energy, you can use these tools and tips to bring yourself back into balance and avoid either burnout from too much masculine energy or inaction from too much feminine energy. And if you can do that, you will have the opportunity to really harness the power of each energy and bring them into a divine union.

CHAPTER 5

The polarity between strength and surrender

Surrender to what is. Let go of what
was. Have faith in what will be.

Sonia Ricotti

My yoga practice was a large contributing factor to discovering parts of myself. It also allowed me to explore yogic philosophy, Ayurvedic philosophy and the yogic way of living. I read all of the yoga books and practised yoga every single day, trying to learn as much as I could. I found a sense of solace in my practice that I had never found anywhere else before. I also decided that I only desired to eat plant-based foods, which is a part of a traditional yogic way of living, and have done so ever since. It really was like a floodgate had opened, allowing all of the true parts of me to start rushing back in.

I worked so hard on strengthening and cultivating flexibility in my body, and bringing openness and stillness to my mind. I do believe from my own personal experience, and what I have witnessed in others, that often when people first come to yoga, there is an element of ego attached to their practice. I wasn't aware of it at the time, but that was the case for me in the beginning. It gave me confidence when I saw the physical changes in my body, or 'nailed' a pose that I'd wanted to perform for so long.

But then an injury to my neck manifested to slow me down and snap me out of my egoic state. I was no longer able to do many of the stronger yoga poses; I was no longer able to practise a headstand or anything that was going to aggravate my neck. It was a hard lesson at the time, but in hindsight it was exactly what I needed because it directed me onto my true yogic path.

It was at this time that I decided to undergo yoga teacher training so I could share the gift of yoga with others. Even once I completed this training, that ego voice came back, because I was still not really practising any of the 'advanced' poses or standing on my head. Limiting beliefs made themselves known, saying things like *Why would anyone want to come to a yoga class where the teacher can't do the challenging poses?* Of course these beliefs were not true and I eventually rose above them. (As a yoga teacher the practice is not about me—it is about the participants.)

This experience did allow me to embrace the gentler, more subtle side of yoga, both in my own practice and as a teacher. It allowed me to explore gentle yoga flows, yin yoga, meditation and pranayama. These are the areas that I love and have a true passion for. In my own experience—and perhaps it's the same for you if you are a yoga practitioner—the longer I practise, the more subtle my practice becomes.

You do not need to be validated by your ego through practising difficult poses. You do not need to be validated by strong practices to tangibly feel your prana (life-force energy) in your body. Your practice has nothing to do with anything outside of you. And that sense of connection, that feeling of your internal energy, that feeling of tranquillity: it's all available to you in any given moment. That is one of the primary lessons you can take with you off your mat and into your life.

The reason I am sharing this yoga story is twofold: firstly because yoga takes up a large part of my life, and secondly because there are many lessons I have learned through my yoga practice that act as a metaphor for life, for example the polarity between strength and surrender.

If you have ever attended a yoga class regularly, you would likely have heard your teacher talk about finding your 'edge' in a pose. And if you are well attuned to your own body and practice, when you arrive at your edge, you will know. And if not, cue the ego (we will get to the ego in a minute!). The edge is where you stretch yourself just outside of your comfort zone, but remain within the parameters of what is available to you. It is this sweet spot that supports you to progress, remain present, maintain the fullness of your breath, and avoid injury.

Do you see how this can relate to your own life? Do you see how you can find your edge in any given moment or situation in your own life?

This is the balance between strength and surrender.

Everything that happens on your yoga mat is a metaphor for your life. You can take what you learn on your mat and apply it to everyday life. That is one of the great powers of a yoga practice.

Yoga is not just the physical practice that is widely known today, particularly in Western society. It is a whole way of living. The physical practice makes up just one small part of it.

If you've not yet taken up a regular yoga practice, this could be another beautiful opportunity for you to form a deep connection with yourself.

Cue the ego

I have shared already how the ego showed itself during the early years of my yoga practice. As a reminder, it looked a little like this:

- Being praised for accomplishing strong yoga poses
- Receiving praise for adopting a vegetarian diet because it is supposedly a challenging lifestyle change
- Not always being present or maintaining my breath during practice
- Just generally being known as a 'yogi'

When I injured my neck, it took all of the 'fanciness'

out of my practice and left me with what was important—a connection to myself.

Of course, the ego doesn't just show up in the middle of a yoga practice: it can show up anywhere, anytime.

The ego can show up in its traditional way, by showing off or tooting its own horn, so to speak. But it can also show up in a different way. The ego part of yourself is the part that is not fully loving and accepting of yourself or others. *The ego is not your true self.*

The ego can look like:

Being inauthentic

Need I say more? Being inauthentic is you not being truly connected to your authentic self for whatever reason, and this is coming from the ego.

Non-presence

When you are not present, you are not connected to your true self and therefore are operating from the ego self.

Having an ulterior motive

This ties in with being inauthentic. Having an ulterior motive is being non-truthful, both to yourself and the other person involved. It is ultimately driven by ego, which is not your true self.

Having 'I'm not good enough' thoughts

This one might surprise you, but when you are coming from a place of deep connection to yourself, you know that you are innately enough and worthy. So anytime that you are thinking or feeling like you're not good enough, know that your ego is the driving force behind it.

Seeking external praise or validation

Following on from the prior point, when you are connected to your true self and know that you are worthy, you never need anything outside of yourself to know that this is so. Anytime that you are seeking external validation or praise, it is your ego in the driver's seat and not your true self.

Residing in the ego takes you away from your true self and can pull you out of alignment. It is unlikely that you will ever be able to completely avoid coming face to face with your ego. But what you can do is this: practise presence and self-awareness. Yep, that ol' gag again.

But seriously though, if you find yourself in a situation where you are unsure whether you are being driven by your ego or your true self, take a moment to pause and go within. Ask yourself *Is this really how I feel/want to act, or am I being driven by my fear or my ego right now?* The more you get to know yourself, the easier it will be to identify when your ego decides to pay you a visit. Never judge yourself should your ego choose to show up. Just remain present, reconnect to your true self, and move forward from a place of love and connection to yourself.

- Where has ego shown up for me recently?
- How did I navigate the presence of ego?

Independent woman (cue Beyoncé and the girls)

Hands up if you've previously worn or are currently wearing the independent woman hat. (Author raises both arms in the air like she just don't care.) Particularly in our modern patriarchal society, women have increasingly felt the need to become independent, like they need to do it all and have it all, and make it happen all on their own with no support. This relates to the balance between masculine and feminine energy that we explored in Chapter 4, where generally as a society we are operating more from our masculine energy.

I have had this experience in my own life, and as you know by now I haven't taken the traditional route in life thus far. I bought my own unit when I was twenty-five that I paid for solely. I have never married (well not yet, anyway!) and have always maintained my independence, financially and otherwise in relationships. I have always worked really hard and proudly worn the independent woman title (hello masculine energy overload!).

I am in a long-term, loving and supportive relationship, and I still need to remind myself that I do not need to wear my independent woman hat all of the time! I still need to remind myself that it is ok to seek support, financially, emotionally or otherwise.

When I was predominantly operating as the independent woman, I did feel a sense of empowerment because I was seen by myself and others to be able to 'do it all' on my own. But I also felt pressured and like I could not ask for help when I needed it. And this circles back to my ego coming into play.

I share this story because I want you to know that it is safe to ask for help when you need it. It is safe to be vulnerable, to be seen and heard in your authenticity.

Operating in this independent way does have some benefits, in the sense that you learn how to look after and support yourself. But by nature of polarity, it can also cause you to feel alone, burdened with the task of doing it all by yourself, under pressure and in some ways disconnected.

As with anything new, it can take some time to become used to and comfortable with letting your guard down, leaning into vulnerability, and asking for help when you need it. This certainly was the case for me.

Even though I slip back into the old independent woman pattern occasionally, I now find myself feeling so much more supported, a lot less pressured, and in the energy of reciprocity—knowing that I am more than happy to support others who are there to support me.

SOUL REFLECTION QUESTIONS

- Am I wearing the independent woman hat?

If so, can I soften into reciprocity and
vulnerability, and ask for help?
- In what ways can I ask for help in my life?

Taking aligned action versus surrendering

When it comes to achieving your goals, chasing your dreams and going after all that you desire, have you been pushing and chasing in fearless pursuit?

Are you putting in the work?

Are you working hard?

Have you been hustling?

Have you been doing all that you can think of to make it happen?

Sometimes these actions can in fact be successful in bringing what we think that we desire closer towards us. Then you get the thing, and sometimes what happens is that you realise it's not actually what you desired at all.

Why does this happen?

Because we haven't created the space to have a dialogue with our soul. To listen to its wisdom. To pick up on the subtleties it shares with us. To hear its whispers.

To get closer to that which we desire, we absolutely do need to take aligned action towards it. But you know what else we need to do?

We need to let go.

We need to practise non-attachment.

We need to create space for it to come to life organically, without force.

We need to surrender.

We need to lean into the feminine energy of receptivity.

Sometimes (like often!) things will not turn out the way we had planned—sometimes they turn out even better.

They turn out the way that they are supposed to.

They turn out in a way that allows our soul to grow.

I think the trick here is really to find balance between the two. It is definitely advantageous to put yourself out there by sharing who you are and what you are all about—by taking advantage of aligned opportunities and collaborating with like-minded people. It is also really important to embody the vibration of what you want to attract into your life, as per many law-of-attraction practices (i.e. fully feeling in your present reality how you will feel when what you desire arrives in your life), but be sure not to become so attached to it that you leave no room for movement or negotiation with the Universe. It's not about being passive in the pursuit of what you desire, but rather being open and receptive to what comes to you.

SOUL REFLECTION QUESTION

Where in my life can I create space, surrender, and allow things to unfold as they are meant to?

Ishvara pranidhana (surrender)

Ishvara pranidhana is a principle in yogic philosophy that relates to the idea of surrender. Translated, it can mean surrendering to your highest self or the collective consciousness. What you can learn from this concept is the idea of letting go of control and allowing space for co-creation with the Universe.

If you are someone who likes to be in control, and you try to control and predict the outcome of everything in your life, then this will likely be a challenging concept for you. But it is not something that you need to master overnight; I simply invite you to be open to it. Explore it and see what happens when you allow things to flow to you as much as you do the work for things to happen.

By doing this, you support yourself to be more in the present. You allow yourself to not be attached to the outcome. You leave some room for co-creation with the Universe and for things to potentially turn out in a way that you didn't expect, but that might actually be better suited for you. The Universe is vast and wise and is always looking out for your highest good, so trust in that.

Yin and yang—the light and shade of all things

You are likely familiar with the yin and yang symbol, where it is light on one side and dark on the other. This ancient symbol represents the divine balance and harmony of all of life. The dark side represents the feminine or yin energy (Moon), and the light represents the masculine or yang energy (Sun). You will notice that on the dark side there is a little dot of light, and on the light side there is a little dot of dark.

Every experience, every action, every moment has

degrees of light and shade. The symbol of yin and yang gives us a visual representation of this, with a little bit of light present in the dark, and vice versa.

Each of us has a shadow side; even the Sun allows the shadow to fall behind him. We should never fear the darkness if we find ourselves there—because in that moment of darkness is a glimmer of light. In that moment, you know that the darkness is serving a purpose. It is giving you the time and space to uncover something you have been avoiding—or something you did not know but needed to—or learn a valuable lesson. Consider it as a sacred pause. A time of realisation and integration.

When we find ourselves immersed in the light, we are able to shine in all of our glory. The light illuminates things for us to see. But sometimes we become blinded by the light, and cannot see things for what they truly are. We are swept up in the moment.

And of course the point of darkness is present in the light; even in the moments of light, we can understand that we cast a shadow. We are not separate from our shadow; it is a sacred part of who we are.

What can we learn from the yin and yang symbol?

Firstly, we can understand that there is light and shade, or positive and negative, in everything that occurs in life—and this gives every experience contrast and texture.

Secondly, we can know that there will always be aspects of light in the darkness, and darkness in the light. It's the law of polarity.

Next time you find yourself in the darkness, ask *Where can I find the light in this situation?* Similarly, when you find yourself in your light, you can be aware of any potential darkness, but not focus your attention on it.

If you can embody this way of being—acknowledging and honouring the light and shade of all things—and remain connected to your authentic self, you will have a much greater likelihood of remaining equanimous through varying degrees of light and shade in your life.

SOUL REFLECTION QUESTIONS

- Where can I find the light in the shade right now?
- Where in my light can I be aware of darkness, but not focus my attention on it?

Leaning into impermanence

> If you can do something about a situation, why worry? And if you can't do something about a situation, why worry?
>
> *Dalai Lama*

Ahh, controlling, predicting and manipulating situations to get the desired outcome ... we've all been there, right? You may have experienced this to varying degrees in a range of situations in your life. You may have been there so many times that it feels oddly familiar, maybe even comfortable. I know that has been the case for me.

There have been so many times throughout my adult life where I have attempted to control, analyse, predict and manipulate situations to achieve the outcome I wanted.

Not to be *manipulative*, but just so that I felt comfortable enough in any given experience. I would go so far as to say that was the case for *every* situation and encounter up until recent times.

Not knowing the way that something was going to pan out caused me crippling anxiety, which would often paralyse me into inaction. If I couldn't control the exact way that it was going to unfold, I wouldn't do the thing. It was unfamiliar. It was too risky.

Whether it was a flight I was taking, an event I was attending, a trip I was going on, or simply an interaction with another, I needed to know *exactly* how it was going to play out. I would try to control the environment, the food, the timing, the whole shebang.

On multiple occasions I did not take the opportunity to go on a trip and meet up with my family, because I wasn't able to control the exact experience.

I would obsessively check the weather to see if I could predict what kind of flight I might have. (I don't particularly enjoy flying, which is extremely ironic given that I worked for an airline for twelve years!) And this is just one example of many that I share with you to demonstrate the anguish that we cause ourselves when we try to predict the future instead of being present with what is and enjoying the moment for what it is.

Trying to control situations and predict the future is exhausting. And it sounds insane when you look at it in hindsight. Imagine all of the experiences and situations that may pass us by because we are too afraid to take a chance, allow ourselves to be vulnerable, and be open to receive what the Universe has in store.

Change is a-comin'

Here's a newsflash for you—*the only constant in life is change.* Yep. As much as we resist it. As much as we hold on for dear life to what is, it will inevitably either come to a conclusion or transform into something new.

When we tune into the earth, when we pay attention to the changes and cycles that nature moves through on a regular basis, it can bring us comfort to know that change is not something to be feared, but something to be welcomed.

We are going to explore the cycles of nature in greater detail in a moment.

Change is a beautiful thing. Anything and everything that has existed, and that will ever exist, has had to and will experience change in order to get to where it is and where it is going.

So why are we humans so afraid of change? Because in our dramatic minds, change equals death. Ok, maybe that is an extreme way of perceiving it. But do you see what I mean here? Change makes us feel unsafe. We are biologically wired to protect ourselves in any way possible, and plunging ourselves into the deep end of an unfamiliar pond isn't exactly the way to do it, according to our brain and body.

So how can we get over the fear of change? There are a few ways that I have found helpful for welcoming change with more ease and grace:

- Believe in yourself enough to know and trust that you are doing the right thing. Trust in your intuition and follow it, even if it doesn't make a whole lot of logical sense.
- Be brave enough to step into the unknown with an open mind and heart. Only a few ever have the courage to fully embody this, and they are rewarded for doing so.
- Once you have done something that scares you a little, you will have the confidence to do it again. Just take the first step and see what unfolds for you.

Change will come whether you welcome it or not. So instead of gripping tightly and resisting the flow of life, lean in, open your arms, and welcome change like an old friend. It will be a much more pleasant and easeful experience.

Check your mind

I invite you to now check in with your state of mind. Are you stuck in an old mindset? Are you still tangled in an old story of not being 'good enough' to go after what is that you desire?

Here's the thing; you cannot operate from an old mindset that is likely not serving you—one filled with self-doubt and limiting beliefs that are dictated by your past experiences—and expect then to create something new. It just doesn't work that way. If you're carrying around all of the things that have been weighing you down and holding you back, moving forward in life will be a much slower process (or even impossible).

Dr Joe Dispenza talks a lot in his work about how the vast majority of our day is fuelled by subconscious programming and habits. How many times throughout your day are you cruising along, letting your subconscious mind lead the way, while you remain at its mercy in the passenger seat?

A lot of us are doing the same thing over and over each and every day, and we get comfortable with it; we find that this is sometimes 'easier' than trying something new or different. The problem with this is that, while it can serve us to a degree, it can limit us from experiencing something that could take us to the next level in life, love, health or business. We remain closed off to the limitless potential that is available to us, if we are open to receiving it.

You've got to get out of your own way. Let the light of infinite potential shine on and within you. Watch yourself bloom into your fullest self.

This will likely not happen overnight. It will be a process that you travel through. It takes time to rewire our brain and break old habits and mindsets that we know we need to shed. Slowly but surely, as you open yourself up to receive, come into alignment with your true self and begin to match the energetic frequency of that which you desire, you will begin to rise from the mud like a lotus flower. Petal by petal, you will awaken and bloom into the highest expression of yourself.

Go slowly and gently.

Take your time.

Trust in divine timing.

Trust in yourself.

Enjoy and savour every moment.

Because you will never again be the version of yourself that you are right now. And it will happen time and time again.

You are amazing.

—————— EXERCISE ——————

Commit to trying something new this week. You know that thing that has sparked your interest, but you've not yet explored it? Go and do that!

Cyclical wisdom

Cycles are everywhere we look. There is a cycle when a mother is growing a baby in their womb. Fruits and vegetables go in and out of season. The sun rises and sets each and every day without fail. We ourselves go through change throughout each day, month, year and decade. Our body goes through many cycles internally that most of us aren't even aware of, such as the lining of our gut replenishing itself every seven days.

The main cycles we will focus on here are the lunar cycle, the menstrual cycle and the seasons.

I deeply believe that connecting with and working in sync with these cycles of nature gives us a much greater opportunity to cultivate balance, harmony and wellbeing. We are cyclical beings, and we are a part of nature, so it makes sense that honouring and working with these cycles will support us in the most optimal way.

Our internal cycle, aka the menstrual cycle

The female menstrual cycle is such an important and incredible part of what it means to be a divine feminine being. It governs and impacts the vast majority of our lives while we are in our reproductive years. Due to the lack of information that is taught to us as young women, it is a common experience for women to be disconnected from their innate cycle, and see it as some kind of inconvenience to living their usual life. Sometimes it takes a reproductive health concern or severe hormonal imbalance for us to even contemplate investigating the workings and power contained within our cycle.

When I was a teenager I developed acne on my face, and my mum took me to the doctor because she knew that it was causing me to feel distressed and impacting my self-esteem. The doctor suggested that I go onto the contraceptive pill to help balance my hormones and clear up the acne. Needless to say, I don't recall it actually helping too much with my acne at all—all it did was cause me to develop a warped understanding about my cycle. In fact, it completely disconnected me from it. I was on the pill for years, longer than I care to admit, until one day I just intuitively decided that it was probably not the best thing for me and my body.

Over the following few years, I began to learn about the power of the feminine cycle, and also about the alternative methods and modalities one can use to treat any symptoms of hormonal imbalance, such as herbal medicine and eating clean fresh foods.

Being on the pill can be appealing to some, especially in our younger years. How convenient is it to be able to just 'skip' your period if you're not vibing it that month, or if you have an important event? But it is beginning to become more common knowledge now, as women begin to explore cycle wisdom, that the pill, generally speaking, is not the healthiest option for us in terms of our hormonal and reproductive health.

I think it is such a common experience for young women, particularly those who are suffering from acne or who experience heavy or painful periods, to be prescribed the pill because it is the only way that their GP knows how to help. Each of us as sovereign feminine beings has the right to choose whether being on the pill is the right thing for us, but personally it does not align for me, particularly now that I have learnt a more natural way of being with my cycle.

The four main phases of your menstrual cycle

I'm not sure about you, but when I was a young woman

all I knew about my cycle was that I would get a visit from my period about once a month and that was it. I did not know until my adult years that there were in fact four phases of our menstrual cycle. And when we can tap into and become super aware of where these phases fall for us, we can harness the power of the individual qualities of each cycle. We can structure our life to ensure we are operating in the most optimal and harmonious way within each phase.

It can be truly life changing if we harness the power of these phases, go easy on ourselves when we are in the more reflective times of our cycle, and give ourselves permission to shine brightly when we are in the part of our cycle that supports that.

We as women usually operate roughly on a twenty-eight-day hormonal cycle (give or take a few days), whereas men typically operate on a twenty-four-hour hormonal cycle. It is vitally important for us to honour our intrinsic cycle, and not try to keep up or feel pressured to be the same each day, because we simply aren't.

Our modern society is very much structured around the male cycle. We get up, go to work, come home, and do it all again tomorrow. There is no fluidity, there is no room to move and flow. You are just expected to be the same each day, bursting with energy in each phase of your cycle, but it just doesn't work like that.

The following is a breakdown of the qualities of each phase of our menstrual cycle. The length of each cycle is a rough figure, as each of our cycles is unique.

Menstrual phase

Your menstrual phase begins on day one of your period, lasts for seven days, and serves as the beginning of a new menstrual cycle. This time is often referred to as our 'inner winter'. This is because it is a time for rest and reflection. It is a time where we will likely feel lower in energy, and be less inclined to interact with others.

In this phase, we surrender and give ourselves full permission to rest and nurture ourselves. You may choose not to exercise for the first few days of this phase, or perhaps just do light and gentle exercise.

Follicular phase

Once we emerge from our inner winter, we head into our inner spring. This is the time for us to express ourselves, create, and interact more with others. We will feel a rise in energy and motivation as we head towards our ovulation phase. You might feel called to move your body a little more strongly, and start to take action on any reflections you had during your inner winter.

Ovulation phase

Our ovulation phase is the shortest part of our cycle, generally lasting from 1–3 days, and is referred to as our inner summer. This is the peak time of our cycle for our energy levels, higher intensity workouts, engaging and socialising with others, and getting things done.

During this time, as with the follicular phase, you might like to schedule in most of your tasks that require energy and expression.

Luteal phase

The final phase of our cycle is the luteal phase, our inner autumn. Following ovulation, our hormones and our energy will slowly begin to decrease as we make our way back towards the beginning of a new cycle. This is a time to slow down a little once more, to tap into your creativity.

As you head closer towards your menstrual phase, you may experience some premenstrual symptoms. You might feel a little sensitive or irritable, but you may not! We are all so different in the way that we operate during our cycle. What is most important here is to completely honour where you are at in any given moment.

And so the cycle begins again.

Isn't getting to know our cycle in such an in-depth way such a beautiful gift that we can give ourselves? We can plan our lives around our cycle so that we are in flow with it and operating in the most optimal way.

A little note

Once you begin to really tune into your menstrual cycle, you will become aware of what feels normal and right for your body. If you are experiencing some symptoms that you believe could be related to hormonal imbalance, such as acne, mood swings, digestive upsets or anything else, I highly recommend seeking support from a natural health practitioner such as a naturopath, acupuncturist or Chinese medicine doctor. These practitioners have a deep understanding of how the menstrual cycle works, and have ancient natural remedies that can support you to achieve optimal cycle health.

EXERCISE

Track your cycle for the month ahead. Notice the length of each phase, and how you feel each day with your energy levels and mood. Log any symptoms you experience. You could do this for a few cycles in a row to notice any patterns.

Working with Mother Moon

The next cycle we will look at is the lunar cycle. The moon is similar to our internal menstrual cycle in that it operates on a twenty-eight-day cycle. However, the lunar cycle is different from our menstrual cycle in that it has eight phases. Many women notice that their cycle syncs up with certain phases of the lunar cycle, but this is not always the case.

I think it's safe to say that most people would probably be aware of when the moon is full or when there is a new moon, however the other six phases are not well known.

The moon has been a beautiful guide for humans for eons. We have used the light of the moon as a guide for timing the planting of crops or taking to the seas. We know the moon is extremely powerful and that it can affect people in different ways as it travels through its cycle. We can see the power of the moon in the shift of the tides.

The eight phases of the moon are as follows. Each phase lasts roughly three days.

- New moon
- Waxing crescent
- First quarter
- Waxing gibbous
- Full moon
- Waning gibbous
- Third quarter
- Waning crescent

Just as each part of our menstrual cycle is optimal for different purposes, so too is the lunar cycle. Let's explore now the two peak times of the lunar cycle, the full and new moon.

The new moon symbolises the beginning of a new lunar cycle, the same as day one of our menstrual cycle. It symbolises a time to reset and prepare for the month ahead. As the night sky falls into complete darkness, this is a perfect time for reflection and introspection; just as this is the perfect time to sow new seeds to grow plants and vegetables, so too is it a time to plant the seeds of our intentions. This is the time for us to write down the things that we would like to call into our lives. This is the time for us to dream—to visualise and identify what it is that we desire.

During the time between the new moon and the full moon, lunar energy increases, so this is a great time to take action on the intentions that you planted at the new moon.

Once the moon reaches its peak at the full moon phase, it illuminates the night sky and shows us what we need to release, let go and surrender. This is the time where we identify and consciously release anything that is no longer serving us. This will support us to step into the life that we desire and manifest the intentions we set at the new moon with lightness and clarity.

You might choose to write down the things that you would like to release and then burn the page, or opt for a similar practice, which will transmute the energy of these things.

This is also a great time to recharge your crystals if you own them! You can place them under the full moon light, ideally outside (by the window will suffice if need be).

During the period between the full moon and the new moon, the energy will begin to decrease. This is a great time to rest when you need to, reflect on your life, and adjust where you need to.

When the sky falls back into darkness at the new moon once again, this is the beginning of a new lunar cycle.

It is such a beautiful experience to tangibly see the shift that the moon goes through each day, week and month; it can really ground us into our cyclical nature and connect us deeply back to nature, Mother Moon and Mother Earth. We can give thanks for the guidance that the moon provides us each and every month.

─────────── E X E R C I S E ───────────

Track the lunar cycle for the next month. You may choose to begin this exercise at the next new moon, which is the start of a new lunar cycle.

As you did with your menstrual cycle, note how you are feeling with your energy levels and mood throughout each phase of the lunar cycle.

You might also choose to set yourself some beautiful intentions at the new moon, and write down the things that you would like to release at the full moon.

─────────────────────────────

Change with the seasons

As we know there are four seasons that we move through each year—summer, autumn, winter and spring. Deeply rooted in the tradition of Ayurveda is the belief that we are to shift and change with each season, and honour the unique wisdoms they offer us. (This will vary slightly depending on your personal dosha type that we spoke about in Chapter 1.)

The Ayurvedic philosophy around how we are guided

to shift with the seasons just makes a whole lot of sense! We are a part of nature, so of course we are going to be most supported and function optimally if we can connect deeply to the cyclical wisdom of Mother Earth.

Let's explore how we can work with each season.

Summer

Just like our ovulation phase, summer is the time for us to be outgoing, to explore, to socialise and interact with others. The days are longer and the weather is warm. You will likely feel energised and motivated; you might feel called to exercise more.

Because the weather is warmer, this is the perfect time to eat lighter and cooler foods such as salads and fresh fruit, rather than cooked, dense foods such as soup or curry. If you are a Pitta type, you might find that you become a little agitated or overheated because you are more sensitive to the heat. (I may or may not be speaking from personal experience!)

Autumn

As the weather begins to cool down, you can use this time to slowly dial back from all of the activities and outward commitments that you engaged in during the summer months.

As winter draws near, we can begin to adjust our schedule, nutrition and movement in preparation for the reflective time ahead. You might start your days a little later and finish them a little earlier. You might introduce some warmer foods or drinks back into your diet.

Just as the trees begin to shed their leaves, you too can take this opportunity to shed anything that is no longer aligned or supportive for you.

Winter

Once winter sweeps in, this is our time for more rest, more reflection, more introspection. You will likely feel called to stay home more and engage less with others. This is an optimal time to be including lots of warm, nourishing, hardy and grounding meals into your days, such as soups and stews, and cooking with a lot of warming herbs and spices such as turmeric, chilli and ginger. Alongside this, you could sip on organic herbal tea throughout the day to keep warm and to reap the medicinal benefits also.

Winter is the perfect time to go slow, to take time for yourself, to nourish yourself on all levels, to rest more if you need to. You might take more rest days from your exercise regime or feel called to move in a gentle way, perhaps by walking or practising yin yoga.

Give yourself the gift of a reset and recharge during this time. This is a time of darkness—a time for hibernation, in preparation for regeneration.

If you are a Kapha dosha type, be mindful that you might need to encourage yourself to stay motivated throughout the winter months.

Spring

Spring is the time when everything is born anew. Baby animals are born. The flowers bloom, and so do we. We emerge from our hibernation feeling refreshed and ready to re-enter the world.

This is a great time to gently and mindfully cleanse your body to release anything that you might have accumulated throughout the winter months and are now are ready to shed. You might take some cleansing herbal medicine or tea. You might do some twisting yoga poses to gently cleanse your physical and energetic bodies so that you feel lighter and ready to step back into the world with ease and clarity. You might feel called to increase your exercise and engage in more social interactions as the days become warmer and longer.

Just like the lunar cycle, the seasons are very tangible cycles for us to tune into. Working with all of these cycles can really give us a big permission slip to honour how we are feeling internally.

I encourage you to honour and recognise each season in its own right, and the unique qualities that go along with it. Go out and enjoy yourself on those long summer evenings if that resonates with you. Stay home in your fluffy pyjamas during winter if that's what is going to honour your energy best. That way you will be a whole lot more in tune with both yourself and the current season.

There is a lot of cyclical wisdom within the Ayurveda tradition in regards to working with the seasons. If you would like to explore this even deeper, I highly recommend reading an Ayurvedic book or text, working with an Ayurvedic practitioner, or even signing up for a short course to learn the ancient wisdom that is deeply connected to the earth.

<hr />

E X E R C I S E

Tune into the current season. Research its qualities and how you can best support yourself.

You might choose to implement this as a long-term practice where—over the course of twelve months—you learn how to best support yourself during each season.

<hr />

CHAPTER 7

Navigating the bumps in the road

Difficult roads often lead to
beautiful destinations.

Zig Ziglar

It would be naive of us to believe that once we embark on our spiritual journey, life will be easy breezy, and we won't face any challenges. This just simply isn't the case. However, as we begin to know ourselves at the deepest level, and as we begin to cultivate supportive practices and rituals, we will be in a much better position to navigate challenging times with greater ease and grace. We will be able to recognise the lessons that are being presented to us.

Once we begin to understand how energy and manifestation works in the next chapter, we will know that at some level we manifest any difficult situations that arise for a reason, and we can use them as opportunities for learning and growth.

When we have a challenging experience, we receive lessons that our soul needs to learn to step forward even stronger and more aligned. If we miss out on an opportunity that at the time seemed so important, it is because it wasn't truly meant for us, and something greater and more aligned is on its way to us.

Think back to every challenge you have faced throughout your life, or every opportunity that didn't quite work out the way you had planned. Reflect on what unfolded next for you. Did it work out better for you in the end? Did you survive that experience and come back from it even stronger and more determined? Of course you did! Those very moments brought you where you are right now.

We need to have deep faith in the divine timing of our lives, knowing that every experience we have had has primed us for the next. We should not dwell on the past, wishing that we hadn't wasted time on a job, relationship or other pursuit that didn't work out. We should not wish that our greatest dream would come to us more quickly. Instead, know that these experiences build our resilience, knowledge and self-awareness, and show us that our dreams and desires will come to us when we are fully capable of holding them.

Sometimes when we are in the midst of a crisis or a difficult or hurtful situation, it is hard for us to see past the fog of pain, frustration and confusion. It is often not until we have the clear vision of hindsight that we can understand why a particular event unfolded the way it did. But the further along the path of spiritual growth you travel, the more you will develop trust and faith in what the Universe has in store for you. You will acknowledge the beauty in all situations, knowing that something wonderful is about to unfold for you.

Challenges, trials, tribulations and less-than-ideal situations and circumstances unfold throughout all of our lives. It is part of the human experience. When we are in the thick of it, it can be overwhelming and confusing. We question why it is happening 'to' us and can fall into a victim mindset. But if we can take a step back, remove the emotion and look at the situation from a higher perspective, we are able to extract extremely important life lessons from it. If we don't, it is likely that we will continue to carry the burden in our body, mind, heart and energy field, and we may just attract another similar situation into our life because we didn't learn the lesson the first time around.

Let me share a story of a recent challenge that I faced in my own life.

It was a Monday morning that began a little differently than usual. Usually, I spend Monday morning teaching Pilates with the lovely ladies who attend my classes, but this day was different.

I was wrapping up what was a long overdue, beautiful weekend away with my partner and my family. We walked on the beach, swam in the pool, lazed around in the lush tropical gardens. We laughed and reminisced while listening to my nieces and nephews laugh and play. It was perfect.

When Monday morning rolled around, we took the traditional 'look natural and not like you're posing' photos, shared some hugs, said our goodbyes, and promised we would see each other again soon. We packed up my little Corolla and my partner and I were on our way home.

We are very much homebodies and love our little farm where we reside, so we were excited to get home to our veggie garden and unofficial pet wallabies. We sang along to the party music that I had cued up for the trip, and stopped to get some healthy vegan burgers to fuel us for the drive.

I insisted that we get them takeaway because I wasn't quite ready for lunch just yet (very unusual for me!). So that's what we did and hit the road again, intending to find a shady rest stop along the way to finally sink our teeth into our veggie delights.

We found a few little sub-par spots that we could potentially stop at, but we thought *Just a little further … we'll stop at the next one!* We then approached our first lot of roadworks for the trip home. We had already experienced many roadworks on the way to the beach and had been dreading them on the return journey, but we were still in high spirits.

We slowed down to stop at the red light, second in the queue. I put the car in park and prepared to wait patiently for both the roadworks and my delicious burger.

I looked into my rear-view mirror on my right side and saw a truck approaching rapidly. I said to my partner 'What the—!' (You can imagine there were other words in there too!) And then I felt the impact. I didn't know what was happening. It was all a blur.

My ears were ringing. I was in shock at what had happened. I turned to look at my partner—we were both ok. It was going to be ok. He got out of the car and came over to my door to help me out of the car.

I had never experienced anything like this before in my life. I have had a very blessed life, and for that I am extremely grateful. We had literally been hit by a truck, and we only suffered minor injuries. Something or someone was definitely watching over us that day.

There were so many nuances that day, so many *Sliding Doors* moments that could have meant we weren't in that place at that time for that to happen. But it did. Had we been a few seconds earlier or later, the outcome could have been much better, or far worse.

So here I was with no car, hours away from home. When we finally made it home a week later, our ute that we were driving in the meantime also broke down, leaving us without a car at all. You wouldn't read about it! I was also unable to work for a few weeks due to the injuries I had sustained.

It would have been easy for both myself and my partner to fall into a victim mindset. *Why did this happen? Why did the other car break down right at this time? Why wasn't the truck driver watching where he was going?*

Since that day I have been reflecting on why it happened. I don't believe in coincidences. It was obviously meant to unfold the way that it did, so what was I supposed to learn from this?

I absolutely adore being in the wellness field; nurturing

my wellbeing and the wellbeing of my clients is my highest priority, or so I thought. I thought that I was mindful, but being forced to slow down caused me to be more mindful and considered than I had been in a long time.

I thought that I was aligned and living my life's purpose. I wasn't. Not one hundred per cent anyway. There were some changes that needed to be made to support me to fully live and embody my purpose.

I thought that I had space and balance in my life. After all, that is what I taught my clients, and I had my structured, rigid morning routines that were there to support me and my wellbeing, right? But when you grip so tightly on to your rituals, they become the very thing that you are trying to avoid.

I thought that I was doing things because I genuinely wanted to, but upon reflection discovered that there were many I was doing either out of obligation, or because I 'should'. But the reality was that if I let go of those things, it would create the space for things that were more aligned to enter.

I thought that I was looking after and caring for my body. I wasn't. Running around from place to place, not breathing deeply, and over-exercising are not conducive to that. I was falling back into old patterns of over-working, doing things that don't fully light me up, and not giving myself time to just be.

I love moving my body each day more than anything, and not being able to do that reminded me to never take my body for granted ever again, but show her the love, respect and nurturing that she deserves.

Perhaps you can ponder on my reflections and ask yourself these questions too in relation to your own life:

- Are you living in alignment with your truth?
- Are you nurturing and nourishing yourself?
- Do you create space in your life to just be, rather than *doing* all of the time?

While this experience was challenging for me, it was a wake-up call from the Universe that I needed to get myself back into alignment—mind, body and soul—and for that I am grateful. Sometimes we need a big slap in the face from the Universe to get us out of a cycle that we are trapped in.

We can become trapped on an endless merry-go-round of the familiar, not knowing how to get off. Sometimes the Universe must step in and take the dramatic action that we've not yet been able to to get us back into alignment.

Soul lessons

This leads us beautifully into soul lessons. Some believe that our soul has incarnated into this lifetime to learn particular lessons that it needs for growth and evolution. There may be particular events, situations and circumstances predetermined on the timeline of your life that are there to teach your soul a valuable lesson. And sometimes the same situation can present itself over and over again because we haven't yet mastered or integrated the lesson.

When you're in the middle of a turbulent experience, it

can feel painful. It can feel like you are not being supported by the Universe. You may not be able to see through the haze that has fallen upon you. But if you go gently with yourself, create some time and space for yourself, and allow the dust to settle, you will give yourself the best chance of learning, growing, evolving, and integrating the lessons.

One reason we might not learn the lesson the first time is a lack of self-esteem or self-worth. For example, if you keep returning to a toxic relationship, or keep attracting one toxic relationship after another, it may be because on a subconscious level you don't feel worthy of being in a supportive relationship.

Another reason may be that you are just not ready for the lesson the first time around. You may not have the capacity to hold the entirety of the lesson right away. There may be some further inner work that you need to do, the timing may not be right, or some external situations may be influencing you at that particular time, such as finances or relationships.

Alternatively, you may not be conscious or aware that a valuable lesson has been presented, so you miss the opportunity. For example, if you are keeping yourself too busy or distracted by the external world, and not giving yourself enough time to be still in your own energy, you might not have the ability to recognise when a lesson is presented to you, or what it is that you are supposed to learn. But that is not a reason to put yourself down. That too is a lesson!

Until we do the inner work on ourselves, and raise our energetic vibration to match that which we actually desire, we will keep attracting the same things into our lives over and over again. Alongside this, it is important to be still, to always remain present and conscious of our circumstances and situations in life so that we can recognise and integrate the lessons that we need at a soul level.

SOUL REFLECTION QUESTIONS

- What soul lessons have I learnt both recently and in the past?
- What have these lessons taught me?
- Are there any soul lessons that are presenting themselves to me right now? (If so, take some time to reflect on this and perhaps spend a few minutes writing your answer.)

Trust in divine timing

You might have heard the phrase 'trust in divine timing' before. It makes so much sense when you are not in the middle of a personal crisis! There are many reasons why I am an advocate for trusting in divine timing, and why I believe we seemingly 'miss out' on opportunities that we desire.

Something better and more aligned is on its way to you

For example, maybe you apply for a job that you really want, but are unsuccessful. At the time you feel disappointed, but then shortly after another opportunity presents itself that pays higher, offers better hours and is closer to where you live—score! Had you been successful in the first opportunity, you likely wouldn't have come across the opportunity that was more aligned for you.

We have to believe that we are *always* being divinely guided and looked after. And as they say, what is meant for you will not pass you by. So the next time you miss out on something that you thought you wanted, I encourage you to remain open to the possibility that something better and more aligned must be on its way to you.

As I have mentioned before, we are always evolving and changing, and so perhaps in hindsight you would see that the opportunity actually wasn't as aligned as what you thought at the time. And perhaps at a subconscious level you already knew that you were heading in a different direction, and your vibration was no longer aligned anymore.

You have probably already had this experience in your life where you look back at a situation and say, 'I am so grateful that I missed out on that job/broke up with that partner/didn't get that rental I applied for.' I know I have—many times actually!

You needed a different experience to grow

As the Rolling Stones said, you can't always get what you want—you get what you need. Sometimes we 'get' things that we didn't necessarily want or expect, because we *need* a certain experience in order to grow and learn.

There was a lesson in it

As I touched on earlier, there are many soul lessons that are destined for us. So if you miss out on an opportunity, dig a little deeper and ask yourself, *What can I learn from this? What is the message that I need to hear?* There are always little nuggets of wisdom for us to learn from our experiences.

There was work to do within yourself

Sometimes we hold strong desires, hopes and dreams, and they can take a little longer than expected to eventuate. You might feel unsupported by the Universe, or question whether you are on the right path.

The reality is that sometimes we just aren't ready to manifest our desires just yet. We may not have the capacity to hold them just yet. There may be some inner work we need to do on ourselves first. And that is ok.

We all have work to do. We all have to *do the work.*

Sometimes you just need to get rid of the junk in order to create space and be a clear vessel for what it is that you desire. This is a really great example of a time when we truly need to lean in and trust in the timing of our life.

The timing just wasn't right

Sometimes there may just be a whole bunch of reasons why things don't work out. Some may be in our physical '3D' world, like finances, family issues or your car breaking down. Some may be on a subconscious level, as we've spoken about. Sometimes all of these factors combine into one big shitstorm that gets in the way of an opportunity. And that is ok too!

Trusting in divine timing provides us with the comfort of knowing that we are always looked after. Knowing that something better and more aligned is on its way. Knowing that what is meant for us will not pass us. Knowing that we will receive *exactly* what we need at any given moment. Sometimes all we need is a little trust and faith.

──────────── E X E R C I S E ────────────

Take some time to reflect on when you have trusted in the divine timing of your life. Was there a situation where you ended up with a better outcome because you missed out on an opportunity? If so, you can use this to bolster your trust in the Universe and divine timing.

────────────────────────────

Complete surrender

The Zen proverb 'Let go or be dragged' is a beautiful analogy for the concept of complete surrender. I touched on surrender in Chapter 5, but I want to revisit it here in relation to navigating challenges in our life.

Sometimes we can try to predict how things will play out, and try to control them. And similarly, when we are in the middle of a crisis or something takes us by surprise, we also try to control, to hold on, or force something. It gives us the illusion that we are in control, and that it will be easier to get through this turbulent period in our lives.

You might hold anger or resentment towards someone or a situation, or fall into a victim mindset. When we think about this concept from an objective perspective, we can see how doing this wastes so much of our precious energy. How crazy is it that we do this! It's like swimming against the current of our life. It gets in the way of the natural unfolding of life.

But what if we approached these situations with more ease and grace? What would happen if we actually just let go? What if that is the very thing that is going to allow what is meant to be, to be? Complete surrender. It's kinda scary, right? It is the unknown.

When you allow yourself to tune into the natural cycle that is unfolding, allow what will be to be with ease and grace, and allow yourself to just let go, everything will unfold as it's meant to, rather than being dragged out until it reaches its inevitable ending. It's like that annoying ex who can't accept that it's over. Nobody wants to be on the giving or receiving end of that!

When you surrender, you step into divinity. You align with what is, not what your mind says you should be. You become at one with the Universe. You align with the natural order of the earth. And what could be more divine than knowing this while you are navigating a challenge in your life?

SOUL REFLECTION QUESTIONS

- Has there been a time in my life when I have completely surrendered?
- What was the result?

Peaks and valleys (law of polarity)

It's a natural part of the human experience to go through highs and lows. Just as we learnt when working with the cycles of nature, nothing lasts forever. Not the good times, not the bad either. And you may have heard before the law of polarity, which states that everything in existence has an opposite, and at some point the opposite will occur. I guess in some ways this is similar to the concept of karma!

It can provide us with great comfort during challenging times to know that 'this too shall pass'. The best thing that we can do for ourselves during these periods is nurture ourselves as best we can, and maintain the supportive rituals that keep us well.

If we never experienced the opposite of something, we wouldn't know any different. There would be no colour or texture to our life. It would be a monotonous existence.

Rituals for challenging times

I will go into detail in the final chapter about many of the sacred rituals that I have found to be supportive in my life, but these are the ones that I have found particularly helpful during challenging times:

Presence

Stepping into the present moment, however that looks for you, is a really powerful way to support yourself during a challenge. Often we get caught up in what has happened, or what could happen, making things seem a whole lot worse than perhaps they are in actuality. Even just a few moments of conscious breathing with your eyes closed can make a world of difference.

Gratitude

No matter what is going on in your life, there is always something to be grateful for. No matter how big or small, there is always something!

Take a few moments to write down or even just acknowledge what you are grateful for, and it will instantly remind you of all of the blessings in your life.

Spending time in nature

We often hear the benefits of spending time in nature, and for good reason. Make it a priority to spend time in nature each day. It may only be a few minutes; it might be a whole hour. Whatever is available to you, ensure that you take this time to anchor back to yourself and the frequency of the earth.

We will explore our connection to nature in depth in Chapter 9.

Community and connection

There are times when you need times of solitude, to be in your own presence and energy. But humans are wired for connection, so it remains important to prioritise connection time with those who matter most to you.

Make some time each week to connect with loved ones, and don't be afraid to ask for their support while you are going through a challenging time, knowing that you will be more than happy to reciprocate when they are in need of your support.

Yoga, meditation, mind-body practices

You've heard me speak a lot about yoga, meditation and mind-body practices throughout this book! And although I am biased because I teach and practise yoga, it is because I truly understand and believe in the profound healing benefits—physical and energetic—of these practices.

When we face a challenge—whether that be a physical ailment, or something in our outer world—it is inevitable that this will cause emotional and energetic pain, blockages and disturbances in our body. There are many people who aren't aware of this, and therefore don't address it.

It is so very important that we acknowledge any emotions we are feeling so that they do not become trapped in our energetic body, leading to disease and physical pain. Practices like yoga allow you to move energy through the meridian system (energy channels of the body) to keep your prana (life-force energy) flowing freely, which is the ultimate pursuit.

Seeking help from a professional

If you are someone who is comfortable with working with practitioners who can support you, you will likely be willing to reach out to them in challenging times, and that is a beautiful thing!

There should never be any shame or ego talk around reaching out for help. In fact, I think it is an admirable thing to do! I believe it is an act of strength, not weakness. Because, as I mentioned previously, although we are our own ultimate master, healer and guide, there are times when it may be imperative to reach out for support for something that we are having trouble shifting, or when we are struggling to see the bigger picture about a situation in our life. Oftentimes it will allow us to move through the challenge a lot faster than if we were to do it alone.

Journalling

Although digital technology is a wonderful tool in our modern world, there's just something about putting pen to paper that feels so profound and impactful. Writing down what you are feeling during challenging times can be very healing and cleansing, and to be honest it can be a little confronting too. But I invite you to go there! Let the words flow from your subconscious mind, through you and out onto the page and see what happens.

Recite a mantra

A mantra is a word, phrase or sound that we can

affirm to ourselves either internally or aloud to focus our attention or invoke a particular emotion or feeling. There are particular spiritual mantras that you can research and tune into until you find one that resonates. You can also make your own mantra with positive words and phrases to invoke the feeling that you desire.

One that I love to use when I am facing a challenge or stress in my life is *In this moment, I am safe.* It works really well because often a stressor in our life ultimately relates back to a threat to our safety in some capacity.

Shifting vibration

A lot of the time when you find yourself in a stressful situation, or a bad mood, or an uninspired place, it feels like a hole that you can't get out of. You go around in circles cultivating more and more of the same energy. And what you need is something to snap you out of the negative spiral. Using any of the practices just mentioned, plus doing things like dancing, singing, painting or exercise— or anything that you love to do—will help you to shift your energy, come out of the hole that you found yourself in, and step back into yourself.

Shifting mindset

As we spoke about in Chapter 6, our mind can be a very powerful tool for helping or hindering us. Take a step back and consider whether you are getting caught up in your own mind and thoughts. If you find that you are, consciously begin to shift your mindset into a more positive state. Begin to think about what you want to experience and feel, while staying present to what is and honouring where you are right now.

The ultimate lesson through all of this is that our life is going to unfold as it's meant to. We have to take the good with the not so good.

Ride the highs when they arrive, without being attached to them, knowing that they will pass. Be proud of yourself when you achieve something amazing. Allow others to compliment you and accept their words with grace.

And on the other end of the spectrum, move through the challenges of your life with grace, knowing that they are temporary experiences and you will gain valuable lessons, if you allow yourself to receive them.

———————— E X E R C I S E ————————

Next time you find yourself facing a challenge in life, come back to this list of practices and choose one or a few of them to support yourself to move forward with more ease, grace and acceptance.

Rituals for releasing negative energy

When we have difficult experiences with others, we become energetically entangled within them and with the other person. This can impact our ability to let go and move on from the hurt, anger or frustration that we have experienced.

By fully acknowledging difficulties and taking the time to clear your energy, you give yourself the opportunity to process and release them, so that you can move forward with clarity and lightness.

There are a few tools and rituals we can use to help ourselves energetically release past hurts or situations:

Cord-cutting meditation

Take a comfortable seat with the spine long, even weight between your sit bones, and the shoulders, neck and jaw relaxed. Take a moment to still your mind and body, and connect deeply to your breath. Just notice your breath moving in and out through your nostrils.

Now begin to visualise, take yourself back to, and fully immerse yourself within the hurt or situation you are still energetically tied to. Allow yourself to experience and fully acknowledge what happened and how you felt, and still feel.

Visualise the energy lines that are still connecting you to this person or situation. Now visualise yourself taking some scissors and cutting the cord or energy line to disconnect your energy from them/it, while repeating to yourself either aloud or internally, 'I now release and fully let go of my energetic connection to [insert what you are releasing]. I choose to move forward with ease and lightness.'

You can repeat this mantra three times, or until you feel that you have fully released yourself energetically from the situation.

Releasing under the full moon

As I spoke about in Chapter 6, the full moon is the perfect time for us to release that which is no longer serving us. The full moon is all about release, surrender and shedding, so that we are able to re-emerge anew.

Under the next full moon, write down all that is no longer serving you, and also write down the hurt or situation that you no longer wish to carry with you. Next, you can do one of two things: burn the piece of paper (in a safe manner where nothing will accidentally catch on fire) or bury it in the earth. Both energetically symbolise your intention to let go of all that you no longer wish to carry and all that is not serving you.

CHAPTER 8

Be the creator of your reality

[The] process of synchronising your energy to a potential is the process by which we create new things in our life.

Dr Joe Dispenza

It was a slow process for me to actually grasp the concept that I am the creator of my reality, as you are the creator of yours. All of the positive things, people and experiences, and everything else on the opposite end of the spectrum, was created by me, and by you in your life. How wild is that, when you actually think about it?

You are going to hear me reference the wonderful Dr Joe Dispenza a bit throughout this chapter, because he has done a lot of amazing work within this realm.

I spoke in Chapter 3 about how worthiness plays a large role in the way we perceive ourselves and the world, and the opportunities that we magnetise into our life. I definitely believe that to be true. But there is also more to the story.

I will be exploring the quantum field, along with creativity and manifestation in this chapter. You may or may not have heard of the quantum field before, but I will share a brief overview of this concept.

The quantum field

Within the quantum field exists all possibilities and timelines. According to Dr Joe Dispenza: 'The quantum field responds not to what we want; it responds to who we are being.' And the infinite energy of the quantum field is available for you to use in creation.

There are infinite possibilities available to all of us at any given moment. Some of them will resonate with you, some will resonate with others. We are all on our own path and have unique interests and desires. But the thing is, you need to meet your desires halfway. Your desires are there waiting for you, but you need to align your *frequency* to them. You need to take *action* towards them.

If you have a desire or a goal you would like to achieve, but are not taking action towards it and don't believe that you are worthy of it, and your frequency is not aligned to it, it's unlikely to come to fruition.

Creating this book

The creation of this very book that you are reading is a perfect example of when I experienced the possibilities of the quantum field in my own life.

There was a very small seed planted a few years ago when I began working with a business coach; she asked me at the beginning of our coaching series what some of my goals were. One of the things she asked was, 'Do you want to write a book?'

I said, 'Yes, I do!'

Maybe eventually I will get the opportunity to do that, I thought to myself.

I hadn't really contemplated it until I was asked the question. But it stuck with me, and the more I thought about it, the more I began to use my writing skills, the greater my desire was to do it.

About six months later I came across a call-out to co-author the book *This I Know is True*, published by none other than the kind press. The algorithm was in my favour that day when I happened to see a social media post about this opportunity, and as soon as I saw it, I knew I had to apply. To my delight, my application was received well and I was invited to contribute to the book. The process really stirred something inside of me and sparked a desire to write my own book, this book, so that I could share what I had learnt to support others, you, on their journey.

I sought out the support of a mentor, I committed to writing each morning, and I was making progress. But after a while I found myself taking little breaks from writing.

What I found was that I needed to keep the momentum going, and remain focused on the why behind writing the book. So I kept going, with a few more bumps in the road.

I knew that to take the next step towards bringing this book to life, I needed to submit a proposal to have it published. As soon as I got over the hurdle in my mind, and took some time to lovingly craft the proposal, I was able to submit it. And that is how this book ended up in your hands.

I share this story because it demonstrates the steps we can take to open to the possibilities available to us in the quantum field.

First and foremost, I had to believe that I had the capability to write the book.

Secondly, I needed to align my frequency to the energy that this book would take on. This involved me visualising the actual book in my hands, and including it in my monthly manifestation and intention-setting practice (we will get to that soon!).

And lastly, I had to take action. If I had just believed I could write a book, wrote it down in my journal each month, and not done anything else, there would be no book! I needed to commit to a consistent writing practice, and I needed to send a proposal to secure an opportunity of having the book published.

Your limitless potential

Do you see how there are many moving parts and contributing factors to how our life unfolds, and how we can either attract or repel opportunities and experiences in our life?

We have been conditioned to believe that we aren't capable of achieving all that we desire in our lives. But as you read through this chapter and implement some of the tools and practices explored, you will see that this simply isn't the case. I invite you to get curious about who you really are, and your boundless and limitless potential. Once you do that, you can start to dream big.

As we've already touched on, we need to trust in divine timing and align our thoughts, feelings and actions. And the last piece of the puzzle is this: you need to create space and allow yourself to receive. You can do this by creating literal space in your life for meditation and presence, taking time to go a little slower so that you can recognise the signs and synchronicities, and allow what is meant for you to flow towards you.

Shift your energy

Before we dive into the practices, I think it's important to first lay the foundations by ensuring that your energetic vibration is high and free flowing.

We spoke a little bit about energy in Chapter 3; one of the important ways we can protect our energy is through putting boundaries in place so that our energetic field isn't depleted. Other ways to keep your vibe high include doing things that you love, spending time with friends and in nature, and practising gratitude, which I will expand on soon.

But what happens when you inevitably find yourself in a low-vibration state? It happens to all of us from time to time, even when we are conscious of our energy, and nurture and protect it.

Sometimes things happen in our lives that can genuinely invoke a 'negative' emotion, aka a low-vibration emotion, such as grief, guilt, shame or sadness. And while it is not beneficial to dwell in these emotions, it *is* important to fully feel them and process them while they are present.

This is because if we suppress them—instead of feeling, acknowledging and shifting them—they will become stuck and stagnant in our energetic and emotional body. They may also begin to manifest as physical pain and disease.

You might distract yourself with a myriad of things to numb the emotions. You may go on ignoring, suppressing and masking these emotions for a while, sometimes quite a while, before they impact you.

Practices such as yoga (especially yin yoga), meditation and breath work can be great for recognising and moving these emotions.

When you recognise that you have been sitting in a low-vibration state for a long period of time, it's really beneficial to have a toolbox that you can access to help yourself shift your energy. You will need to cultivate a deep sense of self-awareness to know how long to sit with your emotions, and when it's time to shift your energy.

EXERCISE

Create your 'shift your energy' toolbox. Some inclusions might be getting up and dancing, singing, getting on your yoga mat for either a dynamic vinyasa practice or a deep yin yoga practice, or playing your favourite sport. Whatever it is that brings you joy, brings you back to the present, and allows you to raise your vibration.

Know that this toolbox is available to you anytime you feel energetically stuck.

Gratitude

You might have heard a lot about a gratitude practice lately, and that is for good reason. But how does being grateful tie in with creating your future reality? The answer is twofold.

When you show gratitude for what you already have, it shows the Universe that you are a safe container to hold more of the same. It is likely not going to work in your favour to ask for more while not being grateful for what you have. Only when we show gratitude for the blessings we already have, can we then ask for something more.

Secondly, when we are sitting in gratitude, we are sitting at the highest vibrational frequency. And when we are in this place, we are able to call in other high-vibration things, people and experiences, because we are on the same *frequency*.

If you can sit in gratitude, you will give yourself a great platform from which to step into the next iteration of yourself.

───────── E X E R C I S E ─────────

2

Cultivate your own gratitude practice. You might write down a few things each day that you are grateful for, you might just acknowledge them in your mind, or say them aloud—whatever feels true for you. This is also a beautiful way to become present, and really think about and acknowledge all that you have to be grateful for in the moment.

Manifestation

Here is another buzzword you might have heard recently: manifestation. There are a lot of wonderful people teaching this potent tool for crafting your life, and they each have a unique take on what manifestation is and how to do it.

Having learnt from other teachers of manifestation, the two focal points that I believe are most important are aligning your energetic vibration with that which you would like to call in, and taking inspired action steps towards it.

I have been learning about manifestation for the past few years and using tools and rituals in my life to call in the things that I desire. A lot of those things have come to fruition; this book is one of them. And there are also some that haven't. Something that I want to point out with manifestation is that not everything you wish to manifest will do so.

Perhaps it is a matter of time, as I spoke about earlier; we need to trust in the divine timing of our lives. And perhaps there are some things that aren't meant for us. This is where we need to trust in what the Universe is presenting to us.

There are some manifestation practices that I have found helpful in bringing my vision to life. We are all so different and different practices work for different people, so it's important to do what feels right for you. Some practices that I have found helpful include:

Aligning your energy

As I previously mentioned, it is so important to align your energy with what you'd like to call into your life. Prioritising practices, rituals and activities that raise your energetic vibration to the same wavelength as what you want to manifest will give you the best possible chance to bring it to life.

Creating a vision board

Creating a vision board is a beautiful way to get a

tangible, visual representation of what it is that you'd like to call in. I really believe that just being intentional and moving your energy in the direction you want to go is a huge part of bringing this vision to life. Collate images that represent what it is you want in your own life, and make your board a really beautiful piece of art that you can look at any time you desire a high-vibration state.

Visualisation

Visualisation is a similar concept to a vision board, only it's housed in your mind and awareness. What a powerful tool to access any time that you close your eyes!

You can connect with your vision through your third eye, really deeply tune into how it looks and how it will feel energetically, and then shift your energy to match it, therefore drawing it towards you.

Setting intentions with the new moon

The new moon is the ultimate time in the lunar cycle to plant the seeds of your intentions. I have created a really beautiful ceremonial ritual that I return to again and again each month to dream about what is possible for me, and you can do it too!

This ritual has been the most powerful for me personally. Writing down on paper what I want to call in and seeing it there in black and white feels very empowering—it really allows you to own it!

Your manifestation is yours to craft however you wish. Allow it to be a beautiful representation of everything that is possible for you. Use it as a tool to create your life the way you want it to be. Use it as a proactive tool, rather than in reaction to what might get thrown your way. Use it as a clear way to communicate to the Universe that you are ready and open to receive.

You are amazing. You are capable of anything that you desire. And you are worthy of it. So go out there and get it!

Open your creative channel

It can be common for us to believe that 'we are not creative'. I should know—I used to be one of those people! I am a very logical and practical person (hello numerous Capricorn placements!). I never would have thought that I would pursue any kind of creative endeavours.

And now, in hindsight, I can see that I was disconnected from that part of myself. The truth is that we are all creative beings. It is innate in all of us, and we are creating in each and every moment of our lives.

Connecting with your creative source energy will support you to recognise the endless possibilities that are available to you, because you have the ability to create anything that you desire!

Once I opened myself up to creativity, and acknowledged that *I am* a creative being, what do you think happened? Creativity began to flow.

Creativity doesn't need to be expressed in the 'traditional' sense, be it painting, drawing, dancing or even writing. (Although it can be those things if that is what resonates for you!). Creativity can be anything that you want it to be. It can look, feel and be expressed any way that *you* want it to.

The way that I like to express creativity is through writing, finding beauty and art in all things, and being intentional with what I do. This can be in something as simple as brewing a cup of loose-leaf herbal tea, watching the herbs swirl around in a beautiful dance. Or writing in a poetic way in my journal. Or even just creating beautiful images for my social media. It's all art. It's all beauty. It's all creativity.

How do you express your creativity? Do you create space for it? Do you allow it to flow through you? Do you welcome creativity when it wants to flow?

What I have found is that creativity is not always on tap when I 'need' it to be. Part of the work I have offered in recent times has been supporting others with some creative projects within their business. This is one example of when I have needed to tap into my creativity and it has not always been available. I do believe that for the most part we need to allow creative energy to flow organically, rather than trying to force it.

So what can we do if we find that our creativity is lacking, or that our creative channel seems to be a little bit blocked or stagnant? The answer is to seek inspiration! Seek it outside of your usual parameters. This might mean trying a new hobby, going someplace you've never been before, or doing something that takes you out of your comfort zone. Whatever allows you to feel inspired, use that as one of your go-to tools for connecting back to your creative source.

As mentioned earlier, I believe that finding beauty in things can spark creativity too. This might mean dressing up in some beautiful clothing, placing some beautiful fresh flowers in your space, or using some beautiful essential oils. Finding a connection to all things that are beautiful will support you in cultivating creativity.

When you open your creative channel, you open yourself up to all possibilities. You might even receive something that you weren't expecting—something better and more aligned than you had imagined.

SOUL REFLECTION QUESTIONS

Journal prompts to connect to your creativity.

- How can I open and connect to my creative channel?
- How can I regularly nurture my creativity as a way to cultivate more beauty in my life, and consequently create and manifest all that I desire?
- How can I support myself to be a clear channel for my creativity?

Connecting to your womb space

The womb of a woman is the most fertile and creative space there is. After all, this is where we produce new life, which is the ultimate creation. But the womb is not only reserved for developing new physical life; it is also the home of our creativity. This is where we find our sacral chakra, which represents sensuality, sexuality, reproduction and creativity.

Tapping into the wisdom of your womb is a really powerful way to cultivate creativity. In many ways, we women can be very disconnected from our womb space, and often have never been told of the immense power and creative force that lies within it. Similarly, if you have held yourself back from expressing sexuality, sensuality or creativity, this could also impact your connection to your womb and its creative power.

There could be some healing that needs to be done within your womb space, and this is available for you to explore should you desire to. Our womb remembers all that we have been through, so if for example you experienced a traumatic birth or sexual abuse, this will be stored within your womb space.

You can see how we are potentially carrying in our womb emotional blockages or energetic cords that are attached to others via our previous experiences. If womb healing is something you feel could be supportive for you, seek out an experienced womb healer either in your area or online for help with this.

Other ways to support your connection to your womb space include:

Cultivating more feminine energy

Your womb emanates your feminine essence, so cultivating more feminine energy will really support you with connecting to your womb space. You can use the practices from Chapter 4 to support yourself with this.

Womb and throat chakra practise

Your womb is energetically connected to the energy centre in the throat (Vishuddha), so doing practices that move sound through your throat, like chanting, is a really powerful way to open up the flow of energy

Womb yoga practise

Practise yoga poses that open up this area of the physical body. Think lots of hip-openers and poses that stimulate the sacral chakra.

Sacral chakra meditation

Our sacral chakra (Svadhisthana) is the home of our sensuality, sexuality and creativity. It is located in the womb space just below the navel, and represented by the colour orange. Use this meditation when you want to connect to these energies and your divine feminine essence.

Take a comfortable seat with the spine long, even weight between your sit bones, and the shoulders, neck and jaw relaxed. Take a moment to still your mind and body, and connect deeply to your breath. Just notice your breath moving in and out through your nostrils.

Bring your awareness to your sacral chakra. Visualise an orange glowing light. Connect deeply with the energy in this centre; start to tune into your sensuality, sexuality and creativity. Notice what thoughts and emotions begin to arise for you.

Have the intention of re-energising and balancing your feminine energy, and your sacral chakra.

Stay in this meditative state for as long as you need to.

When you are ready, you can slowly begin to bring yourself back out of your meditation.

If any messages, thoughts or feelings arose for you, please take the time to write them down if you feel called to. Otherwise, just hold them in your awareness.

—————— E X E R C I S E ——————

Start to visualise the life that you desire. No desire is too big or too small. Your visualisation practice can look any way that you choose.

You might daydream about what you want your future to look like. You might incorporate this into your meditation practice, and see your desires in your third eye.

Remember that the visualisation practice alone will likely not bring all of your desires to life: you need to energetically match your desires and take action.

CHAPTER 9

Mother Earth, the ultimate creator

Walk as if you were kissing the
earth with your feet.

Thich Nhat Hahn

I often wonder, how did we become so disconnected from ourselves, our true nature, the divine feminine spirit, and Mother Earth herself? How did we become so disconnected from where our food comes from, the seasonal shifts, cycles of nature, and what it feels like to kiss the earth with our bare feet?

Because I am fortunate enough where I live to be surrounded by nature, I have a beautiful opportunity to observe how the local ecosystem is interacting each day. There is a lot for us to learn from Mother Earth, and from observing the cycles of nature that unfold around us each day if we are present enough to notice them.

There are deaths and rebirths occurring regularly. There are play fights between the animals. Spiders build their webs that glisten in the sunlight. The sun and moon rise and fall each day. The plants grow new shoots and the flowers bloom, as the dead leaves fall away and dissolve back into the earth. Sometimes there's sun, rain or wind.

This serves as a reminder of the impermanence of all things. And the cyclical nature of all things that are a part of the existence of Mother Earth. The natural unfolding of what is, and what will be.

I encourage you to observe animals and plants in nature. They aren't thinking about what it is that they should be doing next. They aren't worried about whether or not they are doing something the right way. They aren't concerned about what the animal or plant next to them might be thinking about them, or what the other animal or plant is doing. They just are. They just do. Imagine if we could start to emulate this more in our own lives.

We have befriended some wallabies on our property that often hang around close to the house, and they have been such great teachers. They sleep and eat when they need to. They have play fights with one another. They have their own personalities and their own little rituals that they practise. They are present in each moment.

Oh, what a delightful existence it would be if our lives were so simple and uncomplicated!

There is something exquisitely beautiful in the way that nature operates—the simultaneous simplicity and perfection. One of my favourite quotes is by Lao Tzu:

'Nature does not hurry, yet everything is accomplished.'

When we begin to observe nature, we can understand that there is no need to rush. There is no need for force. There is no need to be in a constant state of anticipation, waiting for the next thing. There is no need for unnecessary complications.

If we can lean further into trust, presence, simplicity and surrender, we will begin to cultivate a life that is a lot more pleasant and easeful. Alongside this, we can practise deep love and reverence for Mother Earth and all that she provides us, recognising that she is our ultimate teacher and the ultimate creator.

The right environment supports us to bloom

There's a quote by Alexander den Heijer that goes 'When a flower doesn't bloom, you fix the environment in which it grows, not the flower'.

I remember an example of this that embedded in my mind following a downpour of rain. After just three days of rain, all of our grass, flowers, trees and veggie plants came back to life, looking vibrant, strong and green again. It got me thinking about how this translates to us as humans: when given the right amount of love and nourishment, we are able to bloom into our full potential.

As much as we are the creators of our own realities, there's no denying that our external environment can have a significant impact on our lives and how we are feeling. Let's take a look at some examples.

If you are in a toxic work environment where people complain about each other, the work or the environment, have a negative mindset or bring their moods to work, this will likely have a negative impact on you and your energy. Or if you know that you want to be doing something different or something with more meaning in your life, but you are not surrounded by the same uplifting energy, it can sometimes be difficult to maintain your own enthusiasm.

If you are in a toxic relationship or friendship where you are not supported, uplifted or made to feel worthy, and the person is just constantly taking from you and giving nothing in return, that is not a supportive environment for you to be in. You are not supported to flourish and grow. These people aren't expanders in your life; instead they are hindering your opportunity to bloom into your fullest potential.

As the saying goes, we are the sum of the five people we spend the most time with, and we need to understand the impact of this. Our energy is precious, which means we must be mindful about who we let into our energetic field. You need to be intentional about who you spend your time and energy with. It is important to surround yourself with like-minded people; those who are going to support you in the way you support them, and who will respect your loving boundaries as you do theirs.

Another very important environment for us to consider is our home. If we want to live in a place where the sun is always shining, but currently live somewhere that is often rainy and cold, that is going to affect us. If we want to live on a property with wide open spaces, or at least a backyard, but are currently living in an apartment block, that is going to affect us. Incorporating individualised, supportive elements in your home will provide you with a loving base from which to thrive.

Take a look at the environment that surrounds you at present. This includes where you live, where you work, the people you surround yourself with, and how you nourish your body. Take a look at all environmental factors that could be impacting how you are feeling and the way you are showing up in the world.

Ask yourself if the various environmental factors in your current life align with you. Are they going to support you to grow into the best version of yourself? If the answer is no, you can take the time to identify what changes you need to make that will enable you to thrive and shine.

If there are a few, or quite a few things that you feel that you need to change, you can prioritise them and slowly move through them one by one so that it doesn't become overwhelming.

Sometimes all we really need is to shift and change our external environment to support ourselves to grow into our fullest potential.

—————— E X E R C I S E ——————

Do an audit on all of the environments that you spend the most time in. Your home, workplace, geographical location, and the landscape of your relationships too. Be honest with yourself and ask, 'Is this the most supportive environment for me to be in?' If the answer is no, how can you begin to make some changes to create the most supportive environment for yourself, and what steps can you take to implement this?

It might be as simple as changing the LED light bulbs in your lounge room to a soft glowing light. Or perhaps you need to start spending your lunch break outdoors in the sun, instead of sitting at your desk trying to eat while working.

Notice what arrives for you when you do this audit.

Lessons from Mother Earth

If you become quiet and observe the way that Mother Earth holds herself, there are many lessons to be learned. Nothing is rushed, forced or forgotten. No act is too big or too small. Nothing is out of place. It is all perfection, even in the imperfections.

When I began compiling a list of the wisdom I have learned from Mother Nature, I found it was quite extensive, to the point where I couldn't include them all in this book! Read on for some beautiful foundational lessons that I believe can all serve us.

Keep it simple

We humans like to overcomplicate things, don't we! When we turn to nature, we see that there are not too many things we need to truly thrive and flourish. And although there perhaps are some aspects that are a little more 'complicated' in nature, kind of like the intricate workings of our human bodies, they are still core, necessary functions, rather than superfluous ones.

When you make things more complicated than they need to be, overthink things, or worry what other people think about you, all you are doing is draining your life-force energy, costing yourself your precious time, and confusing yourself.

If we could all lean into simplicity, I think we would collectively be far better off.

Use your intuition and logic to guide you, do what feels good and right to you, stand solid in your belief in yourself and you won't go wrong.

Take only what you need and give back

In our modern society, there is quite a lot of materialism and greed. Sure, it is nice to have nice things and the resources that you need to support yourself and your family. But when these things and resources become the driving force behind all of your actions, it can become detrimental.

The Sanskrit word *aparigraha* translates to non-attachment or non-greed and aligns with this concept perfectly. Taking more than we need, or 'hoarding', in essence means we are stealing from the earth.

Take only what you need and give back as much as you can, and embody the essence of reciprocity. Do things because you want to, and not because you want a particular outcome or have an ulterior motive. Set your intention, but release control and do not grip so tightly to the outcome; rather, become non-attached and open to receive what is meant for you.

Embrace the cycles

We have already touched on cyclical wisdom in Chapter 6: this could potentially be the greatest lesson to learn from nature. Everything in nature goes through a cycle or sequence. There is death and rebirth each and every day. When something goes through a death and decay, it breaks down and returns to the earth, and creates space for something new to grow and flourish.

It is the same in our lives. There are many things that are a permanent part of our life and go through these shifts and changes, only to return to the beginning to start afresh. There are also things and experiences that only go through one cycle and come to a conclusion. Both are perfect.

Whatever unfolds, we can trust in the cycle that is presented and accept with grace that it is unfolding in the way that it should.

Be adaptable and resilient

Where better to look than Mother Nature for a demonstration of adaptability and resilience. How many times have you seen a tree or plant that has sprouted through a crack in the concrete, or new shoots growing from a tree stump that has been burnt or cut down? Nature always finds a way to adapt and shows great resilience, no matter the external environment. Nature displays determination and the willingness to thrive and grow.

Sometimes in our life we will be thrown a curve ball or challenge that requires us to be pliable and adaptable, and show resilience in the face of adversity. When this happens, you can use this wisdom from nature to move forward, knowing that you can in fact handle whatever may arise for you; you can survive and thrive!

Shine in all of your glory

When you look at a flower in bloom, you will notice one petal slowly unfolding after another. It blooms in its own time, at a pace that will likely be different to the flower next to it. But it is not concerned with that; it focuses on its own unfolding.

Once the flower has bloomed, it shines brightly, unafraid to share its beauty. It is not shy. It does not try to hide its beautiful petals or delightful scent. It fully embraces it all.

What can we learn from the flower? That we are all unique, unfolding and blossoming in our own time.

How can you stand tall and proud, and shine your light

brightly into the world?

This is not to buy into the ego, but rather show pride in yourself and your gifts, and share them with the world. In doing so, you inspire others to do the same.

Continue to grow

If you allow yourself to, you can continue to grow and evolve throughout your life. There are no limits!

Just as a flower or plant continues to grow and thrive when in the right environment, you too shall continue to grow, unafraid to reach greater heights, basking in your own glory. Every experience and lesson can propel you forward into the next phase of growth, the next iteration of yourself.

Practise patience and tend to yourself

Patience is a virtue that I struggle with sometimes! However, it is one thing that I am working on embodying after observing the natural order of nature. You will never see a crop rushing to germinate, sprout and produce. You will never see a flower hurrying to bloom so that it can get on with reproducing. It follows its natural and instinctive process, unaffected by any external influences or perceived pressures.

Make it a priority to tend to yourself as the metaphoric garden. Nourish yourself with fresh food, clean water and mindful movement, all while nourishing your energetic field first.

Practise patience and trust in the unfolding of your life. All that is meant for you will come to you.

Abundance is available to all

If there is ever a moment you are feeling a sense of lack, all you need to do is turn to nature. When you look at nature, you will see that there is always enough. There is so much abundance available to us at every moment.

Think of the tiny seeds within a tomato. Each one of those seeds can grow a whole new tomato plant, which would then produce a bunch of tomatoes that also contain many seeds that can grow a whole tomato plant. How much overflowing abundance is that!

We really do not need lots of external fancy things to make us feel abundant, supported or happy. If you struggle with this, I would do some journalling around what is potentially blocking you from feeling abundant.

Do you need to shift your mindset and practise gratitude for all that you have in your life? Do you need to be more resourceful with what you do have?

Notice what comes up for you and see how you can move into an abundance mindset.

Cultivate solid foundations

If the soil in a garden is not tended to, and if the plants do not have strong root systems, it is less likely that the plants will thrive. It is the same with us. We need to set ourselves up with a solid foundation.

If you can lay the foundation of wholesome wellness—mind, body and soul—it will give you the greatest opportunity to flourish.

This is a multifaceted exercise, as we have discussed throughout this book, and is unique to all of us. Discover what it is that you need to do to set your foundations, and then be committed to them each and every day.

Everything is interconnected

When you observe nature, you will notice how interconnected everything is. There is a whole ecosystem even within the soil that we don't usually see, but it is still a vital part of the entire process. Flowers produce nectar and pollen that attract bees, which in turn assist with the pollination process. This is just one example of how interconnected all things are.

Think about this in your own life and the actions that you take. *Everything*—every thought, every action, every inaction—has an effect. Whether you nourish yourself or not. Whether you have a positive mindset or not. Whether your environments and relationships are supportive or not. It all has an impact on the delicate ecosystem that is your being, as well as the people around you, and the collective.

Being mindful, intentional and observant will support you in creating more flow and awareness in whatever you do.

EXERCISE

What lessons have you learned from Mother Earth? If this is not something you have contemplated before, I invite you to take some time in meditation or with your journal to consider what lessons may have presented themselves when you have paid attention to the wisdom of the earth.

Take these lessons and incorporate them into your life, and use them as an anchor when you lose faith in everything working out as it's meant to.

Connection to Mother Earth

It's pretty safe to say that in our modern world we are nowhere near as connected to the earth as we were in previous times. Before the increase in technology, the bustling city lifestyle and our materialistic ways, we had much simpler lives and a deep connection with Mother Earth, our ultimate creator.

Without Mother Earth, we would not exist. She is us, and we are her. A connection to the earth is a connection to ourselves. We are intertwined in a divine union. She never wavers in this union, but we do. She continues to provide us with all of the abundance we could ever need, and yet there is a lack of reciprocity.

So often we don't even acknowledge her. We don't care

for her. We use and abuse her. Like a toxic relationship.

How did we get here? How did we allow this disconnect from our divine Mother to happen?

I think the answer is multifaceted, a discussion for another time, but as long as we can recognise this, we can begin to change it.

What is your connection to the earth? Do you treat her with love, kindness and respect? Or perhaps the opposite of that? Place no judgement on yourself for the answer; just observe.

Some ways that we can all be more mindful about our impact on the earth include:

Knowing where your food comes from

Is your food organic? Or were pesticides sprayed on it that harm both yourself and the earth?

Maybe you could consider growing some of your own vegetables. It's such a beautiful experience planting a seed, watching it grow and then picking it fresh, straight from the garden. It sounds simple, but I am always in awe.

When we buy food from the shop, we can become very unaware of the entire life cycle that each piece of produce has to go through before it arrives on our plate. There is something so beautiful about harvesting a vegetable, fruit or herb that you have lovingly planted and tended to yourself.

Consuming less 'stuff'

Are you mindful of how much 'stuff' you consume and how your actions impact the earth? Maybe you need to eliminate single-use plastics, travel more mindfully, eat less meat, recycle, and use glass and steel storage containers instead of plastic.

There are a myriad of ways that we can reduce our impact on the earth, should we choose to take a little extra time and consideration.

Being more resourceful

Can you be more resourceful and self-sufficient in your life? Perhaps you could be more mindful of your water consumption and food waste, and install a water tank and compost. Work with whatever is within your means. It doesn't have to be a large and expensive exercise, and every little bit counts.

How can you strengthen your connection with the earth?

Strengthening our connection with the earth will be different for all of us, as it is important to do what resonates with you. But some of the ways that I have found supportive include:

Earthing

Earthing can be as simple as placing your bare feet on the earth. This will harmonise your energetic body and bring you into alignment with the earth's resonance.

Other ways you could do this include swimming in the ocean or placing your palms on a tree.

There are also some modern products you can use to simulate this resonance, but personally I think there's nothing better than being heart to heart with the earth.

Spending time in the sun

We have been led to believe that spending time in the sun is somehow detrimental to our health, when in fact it is the opposite of that. The sun is our life giver. The sun is a powerful source of energy that we as humans, and the earth at large, cannot live without.

Of course, it is wise to spend only as much time in the sun as is right for you. We all have different skin tones and tolerance to the sun. But do not be afraid to bask in the glory of the sun, even if it is only for a few minutes a day.

Consuming food that has come directly from the earth

Commercial farming and processed foods have fostered a great disconnect between us and real, wholesome, nourishing food. This is one of the main causes of disease that we see in modern society. Eating real food fresh from the earth, local and organic if possible, will give you the best possible chance to thrive.

As I mentioned earlier, being mindful of where your food comes from is so important.

Using natural cleaning and beauty products

Beyond our food supply, toxic chemicals have infiltrated almost every area of our lives. If you keep your household products and body products simple, you will be a whole lot better off and reduce your toxic load. Essential oils, bicarbonate of soda and vinegar are great for cleaning, while rosehip oil is great for use on your face and coconut oil can be used to hydrate the skin on the rest of your body.

Spending time outdoors

Spending time outdoors has been proven to be extremely beneficial for our wellbeing. Choose an outdoor activity that brings you joy and try as hard as you can to do it every single day!

I know that we all lead busy lives, but it's just a matter of prioritising the things that make us feel good and support our wellbeing.

Bringing nature into the home

House plants are not only beautiful, but have been shown to purify the air and have a calming effect. This is your permission to go out shopping for some lovely indoor greenery!

Tuning into the cycles

We have spoken about cycles a lot so far and tuning into them is one potent way to stay connected to the rhythm of the earth. Another important point is to honour your circadian rhythm, which is a twenty-four-hour cycle that we as humans move through each day.

This cycle includes hormone fluctuations that support our sleep and awake cycles, and is important for optimal health.

You can support your circadian rhythm by sticking to a regular sleep pattern, going to bed at a decent hour, getting good-quality sleep, not watching screens late at night, getting up at a reasonable time in the morning, and perhaps doing some morning exercise.

────────── E X E R C I S E ──────────

Make a list of ways that you can deepen your connection with the earth, and start doing them!

Remember, it is a futile pursuit to have the desire to make changes in our lives but not take the necessary action or make the commitment.

Root chakra meditation

The root chakra (Muladhara) is our first chakra, located at the base of the spine between the sitting bones. This chakra is represented by the colour red. Not only does it represent the basic necessities of life, such as finances, food, water, shelter and connection, but it also represents our connection to the earth. This is a great chakra to work with if you need more grounding in your life, or would like to strengthen your connection with the earth.

Take a comfortable seat with the spine long, even weight between your sit bones, and the shoulders, neck and jaw relaxed. Take a moment to still your mind and body, and connect deeply to your breath. Just notice your breath moving in and out through your nostrils.

Bring your awareness to your root chakra. Connect energetically to your root chakra—feel the energy in this space. Now visualise a red-coloured orb of light at the base of your spine. Feel the energy of the root chakra descending down towards the earth. Have the intention of re-energising the root chakra, and reinvigorating your connection with the earth.

Now sense all of the parts of your body that are connected to the earth, and visualise literal roots connected to your body travelling down towards the earth. Anchor yourself here. Steady and centre yourself.

Stay in this meditative state for as long as you need to.

When you are ready, you can slowly begin to bring yourself back out of your meditation.

CHAPTER 10

Embody your dharma

Each morning we are born again.
What we do today is what matters
most.

Jack Kornfield, The Buddha's Little Instruction Book

Dharma is a Sanskrit word that has many meanings and translations, but the most common English translation is 'one's life purpose'.

We all have our own dharma. We all have a path that is perfectly designed for us to walk down through this lifetime. And this is what we are exploring in this chapter.

In this book, we have journeyed through many theories and concepts about how to cultivate a deeper connection with yourself. And while this is an ever-unfolding journey that we all must travel, it is now time to look forward and consider how you can step into the future as the most authentic, aligned and connected version of yourself.

From this place, you know wholeheartedly that you are worthy and capable of anything that you desire in your life, no matter how big or small.

We all have an impact to make. We all have something to contribute. And this will be vastly different for each one of us, because we all have our unique interests and talents, and we all have had a different journey throughout our lives. Even two people who are seemingly living out the same or similar dharma will actually be vastly different because of this.

You might immediately think of a particular goal that you want to achieve or an impact that you would like to have in your career. And while the majority of the time our dharma *is* connected to our work, this is not always the case.

There are some who live out their dharma separate from the work that they do, and this is a perfect experience too. This might be the case for you! This might look like volunteering, looking after your children, or doing a hobby that you enjoy.

There are so many people who are never afforded the opportunity to explore their dharma, and miss out on living from a place of passion and desire.

There are many reasons why people never discover or pursue their dharma. Some might include:

- Being disconnected from yourself and your truth
- Conforming to societal norms of what your life

path 'should' look like
- Being afraid of what others might think of you
- Comparing your dharma to another's dharma
- Feeling unworthy of your dharma
- Not knowing what your dharma is or allowing time to explore it

Maybe some of these barriers to dharma sound familiar in your own life, or maybe it is something else. Maybe you already are living your dharma, and that is amazing.

Wherever you are on your life journey, you can always remind yourself of your unique dharma by following the things that set your heart and soul on fire.

How do I find my dharma?

So how can you bring yourself closer towards your dharma if it feels like it's out of reach or unfamiliar? Maybe you are really unsure what your dharma is, and that is ok. Some people know early on in life what their purpose and calling is, and others take a little longer. And sometimes our dharma will shift and change throughout our life. It is fluid and will likely change as we do.

So stay open, become aware of the signs and synchronicities of your life, and tune into yourself regularly to check whether you are on the right path.

Keep in mind too that your dharma might encompass many different aspects, particularly if you are a multi-passionate person (or a Manifesting Generator in Human Design!).

Begin to explore

Try out things that you have never done before, or perhaps explore things that you once enjoyed in the past to see if they're still a good fit for you. Exploring new things will expand your energy field and allow the potential for new passions to enter.

Follow your curiosity

Lean into your curious nature. Follow the little clues that are left by the Universe along the way—they will lead you closer towards your dharma. If there is something you've had your eye on for a while that sparked your curiosity, go out and try it. Who knows where it might lead you!

What are your interests?

Become aware of what sparks your interest. What do you want to learn more about? What wisdom do you already hold that you could share with others? What excites you? What makes you feel joyful and uplifted?

These could be valuable clues in finding your dharma.

Trust your gut and follow your dreams

I spoke about connecting with your intuition in Chapter 3: this can be a very useful tool when searching for your dharma. Your intuition is rarely incorrect, so take some quiet time to tune in and see what messages come through for you.

Tune into your physical body too. You will feel it in your body. Your body will provide signals to show you if you are on the right path. All you need to do is listen to them. And that goes not only for the positives, such as being really excited about something and knowing that you are on the right path, but also the negatives: noticing what *doesn't* feel right. What do you dread doing? What is draining your energy? What are you doing out of obligation? If the answers to these questions are taking up a large portion of your days, it could be a sign that you are not living your dharma, and that it's time to pivot.

Your dharma, your vision, your interests and desires aren't random.

Your desires and visions would not have been gifted to you in your heart if they weren't meant for you. They were given to you for a reason, and it is your duty, as part of your dharma, to bring them to life. Trust in that.

Trust in your inner knowledge of what is true for you. Trust that your desires and dreams are valid. They were made for you; you are wildly deserving of them and capable of bringing them to life.

In addition to this, don't hold on to your dreams so tightly that you don't allow the Universe to work its magic and co-create with you. Allow yourself to be open to receive, not knowing exactly how life is going to unfold, yet trusting that it is unfolding just the way it is supposed to.

Lean into the unknown. Take the first step. Feel yourself expand. And watch the magic unfold. Know that the Universe will catch you.

What lights you up? What gets you excited? What does the true you love to do? Not the you that you put out into the world, and not the you that does what she thinks she 'should'. What does your authentic self feel called to do in this lifetime?

Do a free writing exercise and begin a dialogue with your soul. See what you discover. Connecting with your subconscious mind in this way may just bring out some dreams and desires that you weren't aware were there.

How can I fully step into my dharma?

As with many of the topics we have explored in this book, the way we embody our dharma is going to be unique for all of us. I invite you to tune into what embodiment of your dharma looks and feels like. What feels right for you? What is the purest and most authentic way that you can step into your purpose? This is going to give you a clue about how to move forward and fully step into your light.

Here are some methods that I have found helpful for embodying dharma, once you have identified what that is for you:

Take action

Whether your dharma is connected to the work that you do or not, you need to take action on it. You need to step towards it.

While it is true that aligning your frequency to that which you desire is going to increase your chances of magnetising your dharma towards you, you also need to meet it halfway. You have to do some of the work too! This might put you out of your comfort zone a little, but that's a good thing because it means you're about to get something that you've never had before!

Reach out to others and see if there are new opportunities available for you, whether they be paid work, collaborations, volunteering, or interning. Whatever it may be, getting involved in new experiences is a great way to hone in on your interests, and ultimately your dharma.

Seek guidance if needed

If your dharma is related to the work that you want to do in the world, but you've not yet had experience in that realm, it might feel overwhelming or out of your reach initially. You might not see a clear path forward and tell yourself that it is 'too hard' and let your dreams slip away once again.

The important thing to remember is that everyone was new once upon a time. Everyone started right at the beginning. And people are usually really happy to mentor and guide those who are ready and willing to ask for support and step into the next iteration of themselves. All you need to do is reach out and ask.

What's the worst that can happen?

They might say no, and that's ok. It means that someone else more aligned will come along to support you.

The best that can happen is that you start to learn from someone who has walked the path before you and is there to support you in the way that you need.

Be brave and put yourself out there

This might just be the most critical piece of the puzzle. Imagine if you finally got the courage to reach out to somebody, like a mentor, and were chatting to them about your dreams and goals, but said things like, 'I'm not sure if I can do this, but I would like to.' This is not going to instil a lot of faith in your potential as a student.

If you can't believe in yourself and your capabilities and worthiness, how do you expect others to? You need to come from a place of wholehearted self-love, self-worth and self-belief.

In Chapter 3 I shared some beautiful tools and practices for raising your self-worth that you can revisit anytime.

Study if required

Again, this is mostly relevant if your dharma is related to your work, but even if your dharma is not work related, you might feel called to dive deep into reading and studying all the things that light you up and spark your interest.

If you want to change career paths, you might need to enrol in a course to learn and deeply understand what interests you. This will equip you with the knowledge, tools, confidence and qualifications that you need to step forward into your future career, ready to serve others.

This will need to be a considered and conscious action; make sure you have the financial, energetic and time capacity to be fully present and committed to your study.

Pursue your dharma fearlessly

Sometimes when we are pursuing a goal, dream, or in this case, our dharma, it can be a challenge to stay focused and on track, particularly if it is a long-term goal. Situations will come up that can send us off track. Challenges may arise. Opportunities may arise that we think are right for us, but they turn out not to be. Life will get busy. And you might think, *It is too hard to pursue my dream,* or *I didn't really want it that much anyway,* or some other limiting belief. But if you are in true alignment with your dharma, there is nothing that will get in the way of you pursuing it.

Set yourself some clear boundaries and time dedicated to pursuing your dharma, and stay in constant contact with it. The longer you sideline your aligned pursuits, the easier it will be for your dharma to slip away.

Show up in an embodied way

Energy is everything, and if you show up in the energy of the person you are becoming by stepping into your dharma, you will begin to magnetise it towards you.

Let's say that you want to build a successful business, but at the moment are unorganised, run late for appointments, and struggle to prioritise. This is not the embodiment of a successful business owner. Instead, you could make a conscious effort to be organised and punctual, and implement structure into your days. This is the embodiment of the person you are becoming, and shows the Universe that you are ready to expand into the next iteration of yourself.

Don't feel rushed or pressured

While I have said that you need to take action, be committed and focused, seek guidance, create structure, and put yourself out there, you also need to be patient. It's a divine paradox, I know. While doing all of those things *is* really important, you also need to surrender, trust in divine timing, allow the Universe to co-create with you, and allow things to unfold organically.

Go at your own pace. Don't look around to see what others are doing and compare yourself. They are on their own path, which will be completely different to yours, even if you are pursuing the same dharma.

Staying connected to your authentic self will give you the best chance of remaining in alignment with your dharma; remember that your dharma is fluid and could potentially change over time. Be you. Be true. Stay focused on the vision. Stay committed to the vision and yourself.

All is coming. Good things are coming your way if you stay open to receiving them.

SOUL REFLECTION QUESTIONS

- What action steps do I need to take to embody my dharma?
- Do I need to seek out a mentor who can help me embody my dharma?
- Do I need to do further study or training to align with my dharma?
- Are there any limiting beliefs that are holding me back from pursuing my dharma?
- What brings me true joy and makes me feel purposeful?

Crown chakra meditation

Our crown chakra (Sahasrara) is the gateway for connecting to our higher self and divine source energy. It is located at the crown of the head, and is often represented by a white or violet light. This is the perfect energy centre to connect with to channel your higher self, discover what your purpose is, and determine whether you are on course.

Take note of any wisdom or messages that come through from your highest self.

Take a comfortable seat with the spine long, even weight between your sit bones, and the shoulders, neck and jaw relaxed. Take a moment to still your mind and body, and connect deeply to your breath. Just notice your breath moving in and out through your nostrils.

Set the intention of re-energising your crown chakra and maintaining an open channel with the divine and your highest self.

Bring your awareness to your crown chakra, located at the crown of your head. Connect with the energy of this chakra.

Now visualise a white light beaming from the crown of your head up towards the sky. Feel the energy moving from the crown of your head up to the sky, while simultaneously receiving energy from the sky back down through the crown of your head. Feel your connection to the energy of source and the collective consciousness.

Visualise and feel this white-light energy moving all the way down your spinal column, then travelling back up through the spinal column towards the crown.

Now call forward your highest self into the space; invite her in with open arms. Begin a dialogue with her and see what wisdom she has to share with you today. Allow this dialogue to unfold and take all the time you need. Know that you will receive what it is that you need to hear.

Notice what thoughts and emotions begin to arise for you. Take note of whatever wisdom you have received.

Stay in this meditative state for as long as you need to.

When you are ready, you can slowly begin to bring yourself back out of your meditation.

CHAPTER 11

Sacred rituals

To honour and nourish yourself is of
the utmost importance.

Beautiful woman, as we enter the final chapter, I am
going to share with you some more sacred rituals that I
have found to be supportive in my life. Each of these
practices has allowed me to cultivate a deeper sense of self-
awareness and self-worth, as well as a deeper connection
to myself, the collective consciousness, and Mother Earth.

Cultivating a deeper connection to myself enables me
to really value myself. It enables me to protect my energy
by implementing loving boundaries, and taking space and
rest when I need to.

These sacred practices have allowed me the time and
space to connect with my higher self and my intuition,
which in turn shows me my true thoughts and feelings.

It is really important that I acknowledge, fully feel and shift these emotions and this energy to ensure they do not become trapped in my physical and energetic bodies. From this place, I am free to express myself creatively and authentically.

It is an act of self-love to really, truly and consciously look after myself—mind, body and soul. It sends a powerful message to the Universe that I am worthy. And so are you.

I have created a beautiful routine around all of these practices, which act as an anchor in my day for self-connection; this has provided me with the comfort of knowing that my sacred space is available to me whenever I need it. No matter what might be going on in the external world, I have the comfort of knowing that my sacred rituals are always available. And for that I am grateful.

This is my hope for you too. These rituals are opportunities for self-empowerment, self-care and self-love. They are ways to honour the goddess that you are.

They offer a little pocket of joy that you can look forward to each and every day.

Oracle cards

Oracle cards are a tool that I have only come across in the past couple of years. I honestly don't know why it took me so long to find them! I absolutely love working with my cards and I use them every morning after I finish my yoga practice.

There are SO many different oracle cards available today, and there are also tarot cards, which are slightly different in nature. Each card is adorned with a beautiful image and brings forth a divine message or affirmation, and is usually accompanied by a book that explains its meaning.

The most beautiful thing about working with oracle cards is that when you shuffle the cards and one falls out, or you are drawn to a particular card, it means that its message is absolutely meant for you. How could it be any other way? When there is a whole deck of cards that could have been presented to you, there are no coincidences about the one that shows up.

Really, when we connect with an oracle card, we are connecting to the innate wisdom that we have within us. Each of us will interpret the same card in a different way depending on our experiences; you can tune into the image and the initial affirmation on the card itself first to decipher what they mean for you before reading the full description in the book.

You can create a beautiful ritual around oracle cards by making them a part of your morning routine, as I have.

It really is up to you how you use these beautiful cards: what feels aligned for you?

Dry brushing

Dry brushing is something that I have been doing on and off for years, but in the past couple of years I have made it a part of my daily routine before my morning shower, and here's why.

On a superficial level, dry brushing helps to exfoliate your skin and remove dead cells, but it also helps to stimulate your lymphatic system, which can commonly become stagnant and sluggish.

The general method is to begin at your feet and brush in circular motions upwards towards your heart to promote the movement of the lymphatic system. It has also been said to help reduce cellulite, which is really just stagnant energy, so that's a bonus!

If you really tune in, you will feel the energy moving around in your body, so it will have an energising effect too.

This is another practice you can use as a moment of self-care and self-nourishment in your day that only takes a few minutes.

Abhyanga

Abhyanga is an Ayurvedic massage done with warm oil. There are different oils that can be used depending on your dosha type, and they are often infused with beautiful medicinal herbs.

This type of massage can be done by an Ayurveda professional, but in this case, we are talking about self-massage that you can incorporate into your wellbeing routine.

The optimal time to practise your self-massage is in the morning, perhaps following your dry brushing, and before your morning shower.

Gently warm your oil but make sure it is not too hot. And remember this could be a little messy, so set your space up appropriately.

The benefits of Abhyanga are similar to getting a regular massage:

- Detoxing your body
- Nourishing your skin with oil
- Consciously nourishing your body and mind
- Calming your nervous system and mind
- Balancing your doshas
- Plus so many more!

How to practise Abhyanga

Begin at your feet and slowly work your way up towards your head, using circular motions. Apply as much pressure as you feel comfortable with.

If you don't mind getting oil in your hair, you can pour any remaining oil over your scalp and massage it in.

It is best to leave the oil on your body for around twenty minutes before washing it off in the shower.

Cacao ceremony

Working with cacao is another beautiful practice that I have discovered in the past couple of years. Cacao was discovered and used by indigenous tribes in Central and South America. It was considered so valuable that it was traded as currency, and used in sacred ceremonies and for special occasions.

Cacao is a pure substance from the earth and is not to be mistaken with cocoa, which has been refined and processed. Not all cacaos are the same, and you may wish to ensure that you are purchasing ceremonial-grade cacao, which is potent and sacred, for your ceremonies.

It is important to give thanks for the cacao, and acknowledge where it was grown and the people who made it. You should also welcome in the spirit of the cacao, go on a journey with the cacao while you are consuming it, and ask it to share its wisdom with you.

You may wish to develop your own cacao ceremony, perhaps creating a sacred space with candles, essential oils, incense, crystals and any other adornments of your choice. Alternatively, you might choose to sit in ceremony with others and be guided by a professional cacao facilitator.

Cacao is a beautiful way to drop into your heart space, and is known to cultivate heart coherence (where heart, mind, body and spirit work harmoniously). A powerful plant medicine, it is to be treated with the utmost care and respect.

Journal

I have spoken a fair bit about journalling throughout these pages, and provided a few prompts to help you connect with your inner wisdom. And that is really what journalling is all about!

Reach for your journal whenever you feel called to tap into your innate wisdom.

Personally, I like to write in my journal first thing in the morning as part of my routine. You might only use your journal when there is a specific problem that you are seeking an answer to, or if you are feeling really stuck on a decision and need some inner guidance.

There is no right or wrong way to do it. Allow the words to flow through you and onto the page. See what comes forth from your subconscious mind. Use it as an opportunity to express yourself and connect with yourself. Use it as an opportunity to express your creativity and your feelings.

You might be surprised by what you discover!

Mind-body practices

I have mentioned many times my love for yoga and similar mind-body practices. The reason for this is the positive impact they have had, and continue to have, in my life.

In my opinion, everyone can and will benefit from some form of mind-body practice.

These practices allow you to bring your mind, body and soul into balance and alignment. They open the door of self-discovery through the use of your body, breath and mind.

Use the movement as medicine. Use your breath to lead you on a deep inward journey. Invite your mind to become still: this will cultivate present-moment awareness.

There are many different mind-body practices available, and not all will resonate with you. Some include yoga, Pilates, meditation, pranayama (breath work), tai chi, qi gong and martial arts. There are many subcategories for each of these practices, so you are sure to find one or multiple that feel aligned for you. Maybe try a few out and see what feels right; notice the benefits that come from the practice.

Remember that you may not feel the 'benefits' right away. That is why it is called a practice; you need to commit to it regularly in order to get the most out of it.

In addition, the benefits will likely be very subtle, because you are working primarily with your energetic body; it might take some time for you to really recognise and become familiar with how your energy feels.

So this is my invitation to you to try one or a few of these practices and find one that you love. Make time each day or each week to do the practice and watch what unfolds for you.

A little disclaimer here: when you start to work with these practices that are shifting energy, it is possible that they will bring up some emotions or past issues that have been stuck, stagnant and dormant in your body. Don't let this deter you from exploring them.

As I mentioned earlier in the book, it is much better to acknowledge and shift these emotions so that they don't manifest as pain, disease or destructive behaviours in your body and your life. Lean into any potential discomfort, become curious, and feel fully whatever arises for you.

Wholesome nutrition, exercise, stretching and foam rolling

Although this is the 'Sacred rituals' section, I have

decided to add nutrition, exercise, stretching and foam rolling here because *these are* sacred! Even though we are energetic beings, we are in our physical human body form, and it is vitally important that we honour, nourish and take care of our physical temple. I feel there is a real lack of understanding of what it means to be truly well, both energetically and physically, and it is up to us to find out what works best for our unique makeup.

Eating wholesome, real, organic food from the earth, and doing regular exercise that you enjoy play a massive role in your overall physical wellbeing. Adding stretching and foam rolling into your routine is also important, because it will allow you to maintain flexibility and mobility in your body, particularly as you begin to grow older.

It is a fallacy that you will naturally become inflexible as you age. Your body adapts to whatever it is exposed to on a daily basis, so if you aren't stretching and moving regularly, your body believes that it no longer requires that range of motion and your muscles, ligaments and tendons will shorten.

Foam rolling is almost like another self-massage tool that you can add to your toolkit.

Note: Foam rolling will hurt! However, this is a really beautiful way to access the deeper tissues of your body, such as the ligaments, tendons and fascia (fascia is a connective tissue matrix that surrounds your bones, joints, muscles and tissues).

Give it a try! There are different foam rolling tools available that are harder or softer depending on what you prefer.

I really encourage you to incorporate foam rolling into your routine as often as you can.

Smudge sticks, crystals and essential oils

Smudge sticks, crystals and essential oils all make beautiful additions to your practices and ceremonies, and come with unique healing benefits and qualities. You can use them to set the intention and flavour of your practice or ceremony; there are many to choose from.

Smudge sticks

Smoke and smudge sticks have been around since ancient times, when indigenous cultures used them to clear negative energy. Some common herbs and plants used are sage and palo santo, but you can also use local native plants to create a smudge stick, which is probably more sustainable. You can use the smoke to clear negative energy from physical spaces such as your home, as well as physical objects, and you can also smudge yourself by hovering the stick over all parts of your body.

You might choose to smudge yourself and your space before a practice or ceremony, or when you feel there are some heavy or negative energies that need to be released.

Always ensure that you take the necessary safety precautions while lighting, using and extinguishing your smudge stick.

Crystals

Not only are crystals beautiful, but they are known for their healing properties. There are many different types of crystals that each have unique properties. You can do some research to learn more about the qualities of each crystal and determine which ones you would like to work with. Alternatively, you can use your intuition to see which ones you are drawn to, perhaps by how they look and feel, or what colour they are—or you might hold them in your hands and feel the energy they emit.

Not only do crystals emit an energetic frequency, but they *absorb* energy too. This is why it is important to cleanse your crystals to release any energetic build-up.

Some crystals do not need to be regularly cleansed, but as a general rule most of them do.

You can cleanse your crystals by bathing them in purified water, placing them under the light of the full moon, or using your smudge stick. This will allow your crystals to be recharged and re-energised by harmonising their energetic frequency.

Essential oils

Very similar to crystals, essential oils are a natural gift from Mama Earth and have unique healing properties. Essential oils can be diffused, applied topically or inhaled from the bottle, and some can be ingested (I don't personally ingest any oils). There are many different brands that sell oils, so be sure to do your research and make sure they are of the highest quality and potency. You can also research or take a course on the unique qualities of each oil so that you know how to use them in everyday life to lift your spirits, calm yourself down, and even clean your home in a natural way!

I love using essential oils, and I think you will too.

Note: High-quality oils are very potent, so it's important to dilute them with a carrier oil before applying them topically. If your skin is particularly sensitive or you have any allergies, it would be best to consult a professional aromatherapist.

Reading and self-development

I have a confession: I am a reading, learning and self-development junkie! I absolutely love learning new things and absorbing the wisdom of those who have come before me. I include reading in my morning routine. Sometimes it is only a few pages, but it is mostly about setting aside the time for myself to read, learn, relax and be present, while being swept away and taken on the journey with the author.

We all learn and absorb information differently, so you might choose to listen to an audio book or podcast instead. You might choose to work with a coach, or join a program, online course or mastermind group. It really is up to you how you choose to learn, develop and grow.

While I am not suggesting that you enrol yourself in every course that comes your way, have a pile of books that you are reading at once, or listen to podcasts back-to-back all day, I do think it is vital for our growth as humans to keep learning new information that supports us to expand into the greatest version of ourselves.

It is important to fully integrate and embody what you learn, otherwise you will become overwhelmed with information, which really won't serve you in the long run.

Everyone resonates with different people, so make sure who you are learning from is full of integrity and on the same wavelength as you, and embodies what they are teaching.

EXERCISE

Your task for the end of this final chapter is to choose a few practices and rituals to incorporate into your routine. You might already have some practices that you do, or have some in mind that you'd like to try, and that is perfect!

On the other hand, you might be wondering, How am I supposed to fit all of this into my routine? Do not put pressure on yourself to do all of these practices each day if it is going to cause you stress, because that will negate what you are trying to achieve.

You don't need to do all of the practices every day. Maybe you can alternate them throughout the week if that works better for you.

It's all about prioritising. If taking care of yourself is important to you, you will find a way to make it an important part of your daily life. This might mean rising out of bed earlier, or asking your partner or a family member to look after your children while you take some time for yourself.

It's just about setting aside some time for these practices as a way to honour and nourish yourself. Because you deserve to be honoured and nourished. You deserve to be at your best, physically, emotionally and spiritually. There is nothing more important than taking care of yourself, mind, body and soul.

Set aside some time daily to do at least one sacred practice. Make a commitment to yourself.

Conclusion

Well, beautiful woman, you have arrived at the final pages of our journey together. You have learnt so much about yourself, and for that you deserve to feel proud.

You have uncovered your unique energetic makeup, and have given yourself permission to be seen as such.

You have explored what it would be like to live outside of the box—outside of societal norms and conditioning.

You have begun to identify and release any false negative beliefs about yourself, so that you can raise your self-worth and step forward into the highest expression of yourself, without hesitation or fear.

You have uncovered the polarity that exists in life by harmonising your divine feminine and masculine energies, and can now sense when to stand strong, and when to surrender and let go.

You have connected with the cycles of nature, which in turn has connected you deeper to yourself. And this connection to the cycles of life has given you unwavering faith that everything will work out as it is meant to. Even in the darkest days. Because everything is impermanent. Everything has a lesson to share with you. Everything works out in divine timing.

You have given yourself permission to dream of the life that you desire, knowing that *you* are the creator of your own reality. You are a divine, creative, feminine force that can bring forth what it is you desire.

You have created a deep connection with Mother Earth, knowing that she is the ultimate creatrix. She provides so much wisdom and abundance for you, for all of us, without asking for anything in return.

Using all that you have learned about yourself, you are now ready to step into your dharma, whatever that looks like for you.

And you are committed to honouring and nourishing yourself—mind, body and soul—knowing that it is of the utmost importance to do so.

My intention in writing this book was for you to cultivate a deep sense of self-connection, self-confidence and self-worth, so that you have unwavering faith that you are worthy and capable of anything you desire in this lifetime. So that you cultivate a deep reverence for yourself and for Mother Earth.

I wrote this book so that I can place a copy in the hands of my nieces—when they are old enough—and they will, without question, know that they are deeply worthy. They will understand who they really, truly are, without social conditioning or expectations. They will understand how to honour, love and nurture themselves—mind, body and soul. They will give themselves permission to be fully seen in their uniqueness, never shying away from shining their light.

And they will lead us into a new world. A world that values women as they are, in their uniqueness and their glory. A world that is free of the destructive ways of the past. A world that is deeply connected to and reverent of Mother Earth. A world that is filled with love, joy and compassion, and free of hate, judgement and separation.

Most of all, I wrote this book so that you, the reader, can live *life in the soul lane.*

Resources

If you are interested in working with me to learn more about living a wholesome, well, happy and healthy life, you can view my offerings on my website: becrussell.com

Books

On creativity
Big Magic by Elizabeth Gilbert
The Artist's Way by Julia Cameron

On moon cycles
Moonology by Yasmin Boland

Head to my website for more book recommendations: becrussell.com/life-in-the-soul-lane-resources

Quick links

- Find your astrological natal chart: cafeastrology.com
- Find your human design chart: jovianarchive.com
- Find your dosha type: modernayurvedic.com.au/pages/dosha-test

- Discover audio meditations: becrussell.com/life-in-the-soul-lane-resources

Resources for manifestation

Jordanna Levin has written a book about manifestation called *Make It Happen*. Whether you are new to this practice or an avid manifestor, I highly recommend reading this book to take your practice to the next level.

Another great resource is the *Body Parts* meditation by Dr Joe Dispenza. It runs for about seventy-five minutes, taking you on a journey through your physical body and beyond, and finishes with a visualisation exercise. It invites you to imagine what is possible for you in the quantum field.

Acknowledgements

A big thank you goes firstly to my partner, Adam, for your unwavering support, not only of this book, but of all my Manifesting Generator ideas. I know it's hard for you to keep up with me sometimes!

Thank you to all of the women in my family, especially my mum and sister, for being beautiful souls that I am proud to call my family.

Thank you to Natasha Gilmour, my publisher from the kind press, for being the kindest, most supportive heart-and-soul-led publisher that I could ask for. And for giving me the opportunity to have a voice through the written word.

Alongside Natasha I'd like to thank my editor Georgia Jordan for allowing my words to flow freely, and Christa Moffitt for crafting the beautiful cover for this book.

Thank you to my three mentors who were instrumental and supportive during the conception phase of this book: Jordanna Levin for supporting me in the structure of this book; Hollie Azzopardi for being my mentor in life, soul and business; and kinesiologist Zoe Bosco for supporting me to release subconscious blocks and encouraging me to write this book.

And a big thank you to you, my reader. I hope that my words, stories and lessons have supported you to connect deeply with yourself. I see you and I am so grateful for you.

About the author

Rebecca Russell

Bec Russell is a Wholesome Living Coach and yoga teacher supporting women to reconnect to their authentic self, take control of their wellbeing and step into their purpose.

In *Life in the Soul Lane*, Bec shares her extensive knowledge of holistic wellness, energy awareness and spirituality to guide modern women along the exciting journey of self-discovery, transformation and endless possibility.

Bec was co-author of *This I Know is True*, a collection of inspiring personal stories published in 2021 by the kind press.

CPSIA information can be obtained
at www.ICGtesting.com
Printed in the USA
LVHW102104190922
728760LV00005B/189